D0463532

# THE KINGDOM
# ASSIGNMENT 2

WHAT TREASURE STANDS
BETWEEN YOU AND A SIGNIFICANT
RELATIONSHIP WITH GOD?

# THE KINGDOM
# ASSIGNMENT 2

• DENNY AND LEESA BELLESI •

ZONDERVAN™

GRAND RAPIDS, MICHIGAN 49530 USA

**ZONDERVAN™**

*The Kingdom Assignment 2*
Copyright © 2003 by Denny Bellesi and Leesa Bellesi

Requests for information should be addressed to:
Zondervan, *Grand Rapids, Michigan 49530*

---

**Library of Congress Cataloging-in-Publication Data**
Bellesi, Denny, 1951–
    The Kingdom assignment 2 : what treasure stands between you and a
significant relationship with God? / Denny and Leesa Bellesi.
      p.  cm.
    ISBN 0-310-24324-6
    1. Christian giving.   2. Coast Hills Community Church (Aliso Viejo,
Calif.) — Charities.  I.Title: Kingdom assignment two.   II. Bellesi, Leesa,
1955–   III. Title.
    BV772 .B37 2003
    248'.6 — dc21
                                          2002010377
                                               CIP

---

This edition printed on acid-free paper.

Published in association with the literary agency of Alive Communications,
Inc., 7680 Goddard Street, Suite 200, Colorado Springs, CO 80920.

*Interior design by Beth Shagene*

*Printed in the United States of America*

---

02 03 04 05 06 07 08 /❖ DC/ 10 9 8 7 6 5 4 3 2 1

This book is dedicated
to those who have allowed Kingdom Assignment 2
to make a true difference in their lives.
What a joy it has been to watch our church give
of themselves in a way no one thought possible.
Coast Hills Community Church has believed
that we serve a big God, who can do things beyond
our wildest dreams or expectations.
May none of our prayers return void
as we continue to watch this assignment unfold
in our community and beyond.
Thank you for dreaming with us
as we challenge the church to extend
the Kingdom of Jesus Christ
across every boundary to every generation.

# Contents

# Acknowledgments

It has been by God's amazing grace that we stand together as soul mates, writing with one heart and one purpose in the service of our one and only King.

We thank God for:

- His faithfulness in making these stories come to life
- the gift of our obedient children, Brooke and Darren King and Natalie and Eric Johnson
- the faith and support of our wonderful parents, Chick and Lynn Saffell and Harold and Rosann Bellesi
- the continued inspiration of Steve Arterburn
- the gracious, talented, and most timely efforts of Joey O'Connor
- the hard work and servanthood of Eric Nachtrieb and Ginny Leck
- the thoughtful help of Erin Bolte

- the dedicated services of Greg Johnson at Alive Communications
- the patient willingness of Mike Yorkey
- the publishing excellence of John Sloan, John Topliff, Verlyn Verbrugge, Curt Diepenhorst, Megan Rowden, Greg Stielstra, and many others at Zondervan, whom we deeply love and appreciate
- all of you who have made this Second Assignment a pure joy in our lives as well as in the lives of so many others whom we will not know until we face our Lord and King to receive our eternal treasure

# Introduction

We have a dangerous question for you ...

*What treasure stands between you and a significant relationship with God?*

Answer that question and your life may never be the same.

But what could we mean by *dangerous?* Have you ever stopped to consider what treasure, *what one thing*, may be keeping you from a life of significance? Is it a high-paying job? A promotion? A new home or vacation villa? Winning the lottery? Having a skyrocketing stock portfolio?

Maybe it's something simple, something that doesn't even seem like treasure. Like wanting praise or respect or looking like the toned models on the cover of *Muscle & Fitness*. A low golf handicap. Maybe you treasure an Oscar—or at least the lead in the spring musical. Maybe your treasure is writing the next Great American novel or just getting published. Your treasure could be your jewelry or Porsche Boxster. It could be a romantic relationship, a trouble-free life, sex, fame, fortune.

Or do you just want a cool six-pack of beer to drown out what you feel is a pretty insignificant life? A life without meaning, purpose, and true satisfaction? A life without significance?

Let's play this out for a moment: What is the *one thing* you really treasure in this life? We're serious . . . what is that one treasure, that *one thing* your heart desires more than anything else? What *one thing* resides in the secret, hidden real estate of your heart? Stop for a second and think about it.

*What is your one thing?*

Dangerous questions can lead to dangerous steps.

*Signs of significance.*

What makes this question so dangerous and so significant, so potentially life-changing, is that it's really not our question . . . *it's Jesus' question!* And it is a question that has the amazing power to change your life today . . . *that's what makes it dangerous.* It's essentially the same question Jesus asked two thousand years ago to a guy we'll call Rich Young Ruler or RYR (something you can imagine engraved on his cufflinks or monogrammed on his robe). Like many people today, what RYR lacked was not stuff but a significant relationship with the living God. You see, from what we've learned in the past few years, when people begin to take the words of Jesus seriously, amazing things begin to happen. That's why we want to ask you what Jesus asked RYR. Jesus said it

Himself, "Where your treasure lies, there will you find your heart" (cf. Matt. 6:21). Find your treasure . . . and you'll find your heart.

That treasure may not even be what you think it is. As you read, you will hear stories of people who found their treasure to be something entirely unexpected, which became to them a deeply emotional issue. As you unearth your true treasure, you just might be heading down a path to the most significant, spiritual transformation you've ever imagined possible. A life of significance.

*Kingdom significance.*

Right now, you may be feeling a little tempted to close this book. You're a little uncomfortable, wondering where we're going with all this. But don't worry— because you're not alone. You have your one thing. RYR had his one thing. We have our one thing . . . *we all have our one thing!*

This is the amazing story of what happened when our congregation took Jesus at His word by asking themselves what they truly treasured in this life and what they did about it. They essentially asked the same question we're asking you now . . . and it changed their lives in dramatic ways for God's Kingdom.

Taking our cue from Jesus' encounter with RYR, we wanted to challenge the people of Coast Hills Community Church in Southern California (where Denny serves as senior pastor) to take a significant step toward treasuring who and what Jesus treasures. And so, in the fall of 2001, a thousand individuals and families agreed to sell a material possession worth one hundred dollars or more and give the money to the poor. It's what we call a Kingdom Assignment . . . a challenge similar to what we wrote about in our first book, *The Kingdom Assignment: What Will You Do with the Talents God Has Given You?* In that book, we told the phenomenal story of what happened when Denny preached on Jesus' parable of the talents and then proceeded to give one hundred people in our congregation $100 each.

Each person receiving the $100 had to agree to three conditions. First, that they understood the money belonged to God; second, that they invested it in God's work; and third, that they reported back in ninety days. In just ninety days, the $10,000 grew into over $150,000 for the poor, sick, and needy . . . with thousands of lives changed in the process—changes to those on both sides of the $100 bill, the giver and the receiver. Extensive national and international media coverage propelled Kingdom Assignment 1 to heights we never dreamed possible . . . all for the Kingdom of God.

Because of the powerful impact of Kingdom Assignment 1 and the life changes we saw in the lives of so many people in our congregation, along with the hundreds of stories we've received from people who started Kingdom Assignments of their own throughout the world, we decided to launch Kingdom Assignment 2 in the hope of expanding the good news of Jesus Christ to the poor in our community. Our dream was to raise $100,000 by taking Jesus' words seriously about storing up treasure in heaven. And like Kingdom Assignment 1, the stories of life change keep coming and coming.

In this short book, you are going to read story after amazing story about how Kingdom Assignment 2 was accomplished by people who wanted to take a step toward a significant relationship with God. People who wanted to live lives of significance. People just like you and me. You'll hear stories about . . .

- one of the most amazing garage sales for the poor in Southern California history
- a beloved Beanie Baby collection (150 furry animals) sold for the poor
- a couple who led their neighbors to collect *three tons* of food for the hungry
- a woman who chose significance over living with a secret she guarded for years
- a *Surf Magazine* art director who gave up great wealth for treasure he could never lose

In the next few pages, not only will you read heart-warming and spiritually challenging stories of faith, we're also going to lead you down a spiritual path by showing you how to recognize the signs toward a significant relationship with God.

Yes, you're going to read many wonderful stories. Some that will make you laugh; others may even make you cry. Stories of how God changed other people's lives. But our purpose is to lead *you* into a deeper, more significant relationship with God.

Here in Kingdom Assignment 2, we also have a new challenge. It's an assignment that, if you take it seriously, has the potential to show you what treasure stands between you and God (remember, we all have our *one thing*). But more importantly, this new assignment will lead you to the life of significance you were created for. So sit back and enjoy what follows. You are about to experience the true treasure of what happens when God's people take a stand for significance. By the time you put this book down, who knows? You just might be next!

# CHAPTER 1

## A Wake-up Call

It was an early Tuesday morning when I backed my Volkswagen out of the garage and slipped through our quiet suburban neighborhood to my favorite coffee house. Stopping for my morning cup of dark roast is a regular part of my daily schedule, so this was like any other day. Like my family and yours, the rest of America was just waking up and starting their daily routines of getting to work, school, meetings, and errands, and of checking off our lists of important things to do.

Little did I know that this Tuesday morning was going to be different. *Significantly different.*

As I drove the two-thirds of a mile to the coffee house, I flipped on the radio expecting to hear the familiar voices of the sports talk radio show I love to listen to. But what I heard instead was the serious tone ·of a National Emergency newsbreak. The details were sketchy, but there had been an apparent attack on the World Trade Center in New York City and the Pentagon in Washington, D.C. Soon, words of hijacking, explosions, and chaos filled every radio station in America.

With my heart pounding, I punched the speed dial on my cell phone to call home. "Leesa, turn on the TV! Something terrible has happened!"

## America's Wake-up Call

As I sat glued to my car radio in the coffee house parking lot, I listened to the shocking course of events of September 11. From that tragic morning, every American old enough to realize what had just taken place seemed to wake up and take a step back to reevaluate their lives and priorities from a different perspective. For the first time in a long time, we began to question what we truly treasure.

All of a sudden, the things we once deemed so important and urgent didn't seem as important and urgent. Chasing that big business deal. Managing the bottom line. Monitoring our stock portfolio. Buying the right car to fit our image. Shopping for the latest fashions. Making a great first impression. Trying to impress our friends and neighbors with who we are, what we do, or what we own.

All of this seemed to pale in comparison to matters more important.

Matters more significant.

Matters that resonated within our souls and our very being.

Like relationships.

After 9/11, we wanted to be with our families. We saw the face of death and the brevity of life, and we ran into the arms of those whom we love and whose relationship we cherish. We wanted to stop and think again about whom we loved and appreciated. We also realized how much we had taken for granted in our country and what truly makes her great. We wanted to remember and rekindle some of the values that had slipped away or been set aside in pursuit of what we thought was more important. Values like patriotism, sacrifice, generosity, and our strength of unity in diversity.

Church attendance soared. We wanted to connect or reconnect with God. We needed to know He was with us. Personal prayers and public invocations of God's protection and provision were not only welcomed, but also embraced and sought. People from all walks of life began taking a spiritual inventory of what was in their heart and what their life was all about. America's preoccupation with personal *success* was giving way to something greater, something more compelling, something deeper in nature. That something, I believe, is true *significance*.

## What Is Significance?

Bobb Biehl, a good friend of mine, has spent the last twenty-five years consulting with Christian leaders all over the country and the world. I will never forget what he told me about the difference between *success* and *significance*. "Success," he said, "is really as simple as accomplishing your goals, whatever they may be. Significance, on the other hand, is about setting your sights on accomplishing the *right* goal—the things that make life really worth living."

*Webster's Dictionary* defines "significance" as that which is "important, meaningful, and even momentous." Significance is living a God-honoring life by being a person focused on the right goals and doing what is important and meaningful. That's what makes life worth living. Significance is also that deep, profound satisfaction in our hearts that comes with living a life filled with meaning and purpose. Our longing for significance is what wakes us up from our slumber of those things we once thought were so important and points us in the direction of what is *truly* important. Significance shows us where true treasure lies. It is the day-to-day understanding of knowing the difference between real gold and fool's gold.

Jesus talked quite a bit about significance. He spoke often about what's significant in this life and what isn't. He taught the multitudes about significance in terms of the real life found in following Him. To those who dared to personally follow after Him, Jesus explained the daily benefits of His rule and His reign over their hearts and lives. Benefits that weren't some spiritual pie-in-the-sky sentiments awaiting us in heaven, but real, tangible benefits available to us here and now in order to make a practical difference in our lives. The benefits of the Kingdom Jesus spoke about are the benefits that can awaken lives. Benefits that can change hearts. Benefits that He promised *will* change lives.

When Jesus spoke to people two thousand years ago, He was speaking to people like you and me. People with hearts that longed for significance. Whether rich or poor, Jesus spoke to people who wrestled with money problems, possessions, materialism, and stuff. He met with, taught, encouraged, and loved people who wondered, "How much stuff is enough," and "What's really most important in this life?" For people who thought there was no significant relationship between money and their relationship with God, Jesus shook them up by making a whip and driving out the moneychangers. He did all of this to drive home the importance of having a significant relationship with Him. Jesus' ministry pointed to learning what it takes to be in a right relationship with Him and to enjoy the significant Kingdom life that follows in this life and the next.

Whether you count yourself as a follower of Christ or not, all of us want to experience a life of significance. The problem, you see, is most of us are oblivious to it.

I am convinced that most people miss significance because, for the most part, all of our arrows and efforts are aimed at a different target: the target of *success*. While success is great when and where you can gain it, it is not enough, nor will it ever be enough, to sustain the life of significance you and I are looking for. Far too often, we are much more focused on the treasures of success than the benefits of significance. The pull between the siren call of success and choosing a life of significance has been a tension felt by Christ followers for two thousand years. It's a tension felt in your home and in your church. It's a tension felt in my home and in our church. It's a tension so real, so potentially distracting to developing a significant relationship with the living God, that as Leesa and I dreamed about a second Kingdom Assignment, we knew it was an issue too impossible to ignore.

## Count Me In!

The immediate impact of the 9/11 terrorist attacks, combined with the poor showing in the U.S. economy, left many local charities in need of funds. Charities in Orange County, California, and throughout the nation were unable to maintain the same level of care and service to the poor as they had prior to 9/11. We thought this would make a perfect time for Coast Hills Community Church to help the poor in our community by launching Kingdom Assignment 2. We wanted to give of ourselves in a small, yet significant way.

After the amazing experience of Kingdom Assignment 1, we had many people at our church express how they wished they had been one of the initial 100 people to receive the $100. Well, for Kingdom Assignment 2, our people were going to get the chance they wanted. We were casting the net far and wide! We were going to ask 1000 individuals and families to sell something they treasured—something worth at least $100. And once sold, they were to give the money to the poor.

So, a few weeks after 9/11, I preached a sermon called "Finding Significance." In this message, I told the story of the Rich Young Ruler and essentially asked the question: "What treasure stands between you and a significant relationship with God?" Like Kingdom Assignment 1, the people in our auditorium didn't know what was coming next. They didn't know I was about to challenge them out of their comfort zones.

I was excited for this next Kingdom Assignment, but I was also a little frightened. Getting 100 people to volunteer is one thing, but 1000? I knew it was easier to hand out $100 than to ask our people to search their own hearts and find out what treasure needed to go. We also set the bar pretty high. Our dream was to raise $100,000 for the poor in our community, and I wasn't sure if we'd be able to get 1000 people to step up to the plate. I didn't know how this next Kingdom Assignment was going to be received. But like most of life in God's Kingdom, I was walking by faith and not sight.

I ended my message about RYR by explaining the dire state of local charities and that now was the time for the Church to step in and be the Church God has called it to be. Though no one knew what it was or what it was for, in each person's bulletin was a small strip of white paper that read, "Count Me In." Okay, so we gave them a hint something was coming!

"I have a new Kingdom Assignment for you," I said to the people in each of our four services. "I need 1000 individuals and families who will be willing to sell something of $100 in value and donate the proceeds to the poor in our community. If you want to live a life of significance and do something significant for God's Kingdom, all I need you to do is to take that little piece of paper that says 'Count Me In' and place it in one of the baskets here in the front aisle. That is your new Kingdom Assignment!"

Fortunately, unlike Kingdom Assignment 1, I didn't have to collar people to come forward. At each service, to our pleasant surprise, hundreds of people came forward. They were ready, eager, and willing to do something great for God's Kingdom. Old people. Young people. Singles. Business professionals. Stay-at-home moms. Kids. Moms and Dads. Whole families came forward, eager to be counted in.

By the end of our four services, they were all instructed that they had eight weeks to sell a treasured possession and bring the money back for a special offering to be taken on Thanksgiving weekend. A thousand people were now off and running with a new Kingdom Assignment. In the days that followed, we heard comment after comment expressing enthusiasm and nervous excitement over this new challenge of faith. People told us . . .

- This is something all of us can do!
- Thank you for challenging us.
- After Kingdom Assignment 1, I definitely didn't want to miss my chance to be involved.
- This is such a creative way to put my faith and devotion to Christ into action.
- I'm eager to serve the poor. I've never done anything like this!

These were people just like you and me. They came from every walk of life and season of spiritual development. What they shared in common was a desire to be faithful to do something significant to advance the Kingdom of God. All of this makes me think: I wonder what would have happened if RYR had said to Jesus:

"Count me in!"

## What to Give the Man Who *Thinks* He Has Everything

In *The Kingdom Assignment*, we challenged readers to take seriously what God's Word says about money. We asked readers to consider making a radical change in their thinking by understanding that every dollar we have and everything we own comes from God. We emphasized the importance of *using money* to demonstrate one's love and service and devotion to God instead of *loving money.*

In the story of RYR, we see this dynamic tension alive and present in the life of a wealthy young man who said, "Count me out," instead of "Count me in"! We see a young man who wanted significance but who discovered that the cost of significance was far greater than what he paid for all his stuff. We see a man who thought he had everything, but who was in for a great surprise when Jesus told him he lacked one thing. *There's that "one thing" again.*

In the three Gospel profiles of the story, we're never told RYR's name—only his credentials. He is rich, young, and influential. He is the twenty-first-century equivalent to a trust fund baby, an MBA graduate in a lucrative position loaded with stock options, or an entrepreneur who just sold out and is now sitting on a big, fat pile of cash. The Gospels don't tell us where his money came from, but the guy's got bank. He has every treasure his heart ever desired, everything you think would bring him satisfaction. Yet, he wasn't satisfied with all his stuff, and he knew it. He had everything in his possession except the one thing that would give him what he wanted most . . . *significance*. As a result, he went in search of Jesus to find the life he was looking for. It was this story, found in Mark 10:17–22, that we used as the foundation for Kingdom Assignment 2:

> As Jesus started on his way, a man ran up to him and fell on his knees before him. "Good teacher," he asked, "what must I do to inherit eternal life?"
>
> "Why do you call me good?" Jesus answered. "No one is good—except God alone. You know the commandments: 'Do not murder, do not commit adultery, do not steal, do not give false testimony, do not defraud, honor your father and mother.'"
>
> "Teacher," he declared, "all these I have kept since I was a boy."
>
> Jesus looked at him and loved him. "One thing you lack," he said. "Go, sell everything you have and give to the poor, and you will have treasure in heaven. Then come, follow me."
>
> At this the man's face fell. He went away sad, because he had great wealth.

RYR got his audience with Jesus. He was a guy who probably learned early on that if he was ever to be successful in this world, he needed to take the initiative and go for it! And go for it he did.

Then one day, something changed. Who knows what? Maybe he had a bad day in the stock market. Maybe he was looking at all his treasure and riches wondering, "Is this it? Is this all I have to live for?" Maybe he experienced some sort of tragedy or had recently lost a close friend. Maybe he began to think about his own mortality. Maybe he was just riding across town and began wondering about his relationship with his wife and kids, thinking how little he had invested in their lives.

Whatever it was, RYR has a wake-up call that causes him to stop and reevaluate what is most important to him and what is lacking in his life. The story tells us that he *runs* to meet Jesus and gets down on his knees, probably with all the same drive and initiative he has pursued all his other opportunities and ventures.

> *"Good teacher,"* he asks, *"what must I do to inherit eternal life?"*

Sounds like a straight question, doesn't it? But, his actions and words are a bit suspicious. You see, no one ever called a rabbi a "good teacher" because the rabbis never considered themselves good teachers. "Good" is an adjective reserved for God and God alone. Jesus wants to know where this man really stands. Is he really interested in finding the significance that God alone can give him, or is he only interested in adding a little religion to his already impressive list of successes? Is he interested in pursuing the life of significance Jesus promises or does he hear that going to church is a good place for business networking?

Jesus points RYR to God's Top Ten. It's Religion 101—and RYR has heard it all since he was a kid. Jesus rattles off five or six of the commandments for the guy to check his heart.

"Been there, done that!" the man responds. " Maybe I've arrived and never really knew it?"

Hardly.

Isn't it interesting to note a few of the Ten Commandments Jesus *doesn't* mention to him? How about the first commandment, "I am the Lord God. You shall have no other gods before Me." Or what about the second commandment? "You shall not make an idol of anything or worship any created or inanimate thing instead of Me." If Jesus wanted, he could have nailed RYR on these two commandments alone and point out the true condition of his heart. But Jesus doesn't! Instead, the Bible tells us, *"Jesus looked at him and loved him."*

I wonder, when Jesus looks RYR in the eyes, what do you think he sees? I think Jesus sees what this man really wants and what he can become by discovering what real significance is ... what true success is ... what kind of life is really worth living.

I also imagine Jesus looks into this young man's eyes and sees all the people RYR could influence for the Kingdom of God if he would only realize that his life isn't all about him. It isn't all about his treasures or his riches. It isn't about his agenda or what he is going to do for Jesus. It's all about finding true significance by letting God work in him and through him to accomplish His will and purpose in his life.

Now, here comes the crucial point of the story. There's one more thing I believe Jesus sees in this man's face. And that is the *one thing* in RYR's life that stands between him and the life he longs for. When Jesus looks at RYR and loves him, it is love that prompts Jesus to tell him the truth. And when you read the story, you get the impression that the man is ready for Jesus to tell him anything . . . except the *one thing* Jesus does tell him.

> *"One thing you lack," Jesus said. "Go, sell everything you have and give to the poor, and you will have treasure in heaven. Then come, follow me."*

Jesus' "one thing" is the last thing RYR expected to hear.

> *At this the man's face fell. He went away sad, because he had great wealth.*

RYR lacks one thing, wants one thing, but cannot give up his one thing to find the life he is looking for. He sacrifices a life of significance for stuff. He lets his treasure stand in the way of significance. RYR's one thing, his wealth, is the deal-breaker. And it only takes one thing to be a deal-breaker.

He goes away sad, but not sad enough.

RYR has his one thing . . . and we all have our one thing.

What's your one thing? It's a question we'll keep coming back to again and again in this book.

I wonder what would have happened to RYR if he had had the chance to meet a nine-year-old friend of ours? I wonder what might have happened in the life of RYR if he had the courage of a young guy named Collin?

## Collin's Story

Collin is a boy in our church with a passionate heart for God. Collin can't do a lot of things, but at his young age he has chosen to do a few right and significant things. Unlike most nine-year-olds whose lives are filled with baseball, soccer, and other high-energy activities, Collin has such severe medical problems that he has never been able to slide into second or hit the winning shot at the buzzer. Ever since he was eight months old, Collin has suffered with juvenile rheumatoid arthritis, asthma, allergies, and fibromyalgia. These physical complications have required various surgeries throughout his young life and more time with doctors than most kids will ever see in their lifetime.

On some days, Collin has to come home from school early because his body hurts so much. The arthritis affects his jaw, making it painful to eat, as well as his fingers and feet. His parents suffer with the daily decision of letting him go out and play—how do you keep a nine-year-old boy from being a nine-year-old boy? But whenever Collin goes out to play, he pays for it the next day. He recently got to go to LEGOLAND in San Diego—but unlike most kids, Collin had to go in a wheelchair.

I will never forget the first time I met Collin. One day he called the church office and made an appointment to see me. His mother didn't even know he called. On the day of the appointment, my assistant Ginny and I didn't have any idea who Collin was or how old he was. When the appointment time arrived, in walks this little boy. He wasn't even tall enough to peek over the receptionist's counter, but he boldly announces he has an appointment with Pastor Denny.

As Ginny led him into my office, in a polite and assertive voice, Collin introduces himself and reaches out to give me a firm handshake.

"Hello, Pastor Denny. I made this appointment to meet you and to ask if you would pray with me about a surgery I'm going to have next week."

*My, oh my*, I glanced at Ginny. Is this the same person who called to have me meet and pray with him? I was taken back to say the least. What I discovered in the next thirty minutes was that Collin wanted to see a significant work of God done in his life.

Collin told me how he and his mother prayed together every night. At the top of his list, Collin wanted his dad to receive Christ into his own life. One year later, Collin's prayer was answered. I had the privilege of baptizing Collin's dad, Steve, in our church when, with tears in his eyes, he publicly shared his newfound faith in Jesus Christ. As Steve recounted his own story, he thanked God, his wife, and most of all, Collin, for showing him the way. How about that?

A nine-year-old well on his way to a life of significance.

Collin was also one of the first to complete this second Kingdom Assignment. When he took on the Kingdom Assignment, he thought about what treasure might be keeping him from a significant relationship with God and what would be the best way for him to help the poor. The answer came quickly.

He went straight to his piggy bank. Call it a kid's Fort Knox—his personal Federal Reserve. He emptied the bank, which served as his treasure chest for toys and money for the movies. Collin decided helping the poor would be a higher priority this coming year than going to the movies. His demonstration of faith was bold and decisive. His willing generosity spoke loud and clear of his love for Christ. He wasn't about to let his treasure keep him from a significant relationship with God and from living a life of significance.

*Collin gets it.*

Didn't Isaiah say something about *"and a little child will lead them"* (Isa. 11:6)?

## What's Your Story?

Collin has his story. We have our story. As you read the chapters that follow, it is our hope and prayer that you will find your own story as you consider what treasure might be standing in between you and a significant relationship with God.

Ultimately, following Jesus Christ and finding significance from His perspective is never on our terms . . . not if we're serious about being His disciples. RYR had his one thing—his money. Your one thing may have nothing to do with money or possessions. Rather, it may be whatever you find your identity, your security, your success, or your comfort in. Living a life of Kingdom significance involves letting go of whatever your heart treasures in order to take hold of something more important and ever more valuable. That something only God can give us.

In the pages to come, we want to share life-transforming stories of Kingdom Assignment 2 as well as what happens when people set their hearts doing something significant for God's Kingdom. We're also going to share with you what we see as the Seven Signs of a Significant Life and the process of pursuing the significant life you've always longed for. We've seen thousands of people's lives changed in Kingdom Assignment 2 and in places you might never expect . . . like a garage sale!

# CHAPTER 2

# *Treasure Sale*

Kingdom Assignment 2 hit the ground running—or should we say, shopping? For this new assignment to work we were in need of some buyers or takers of our $100 items. Among the 1000 participants, we sensed anticipation and excitement over what God was going to do and how He was going to work through each person who stepped forward in this new adventure of faith.

It's easy to hand out $100, but to ask a thousand people to sell an item worth $100, well, for some people, that's a tall order. We knew that people were ready and willing to sell their belongings to assist the poor in our area, and we wanted to give them an opportunity to do just that ... but how?

One morning, I got a phone call from a woman in our church named Linda. In an excited voice, she told me how she had heard of other families in the church organizing their own Kingdom Assignment garage sales. "Why recreate the wheel?" she asked me. Then she proceeded to explain her idea of bringing all the families together for a church-wide garage sale.

"Garage sale," I moaned. "I've seen so many cheesy church rummage sales in my years of ministry that I'm embarrassed to be associated with one. It sounds like a good idea, but . . ."

Linda knew exactly where I was coming from. "I know what you're saying, I don't want to see the church parking lot filled with a bunch of junk either. This is going to be a class act. In fact I even have a new name for it . . . what do you think of calling it a 'Treasure Sale'?"

I was sold. "Great idea! Go for it!"

## Ready, Set–Go!

Linda spearheaded a team of enthusiastic volunteers for our newly named "Treasure Sale." A Saturday morning was set for the big event. We advertised in the church bulletin and local newspapers. Flyers were handed out in neighborhoods, all to get the word out for the greatest treasure sale in church history.

On the morning of the event, cars started pulling into the Coast Hills parking lot while it was still dark. Men, women, and children of all ages started unloading boxes out of minivans, trucks, and Volkswagon Beetles. Even though this was a church event, people were vying for spaces as if this was festival seating at a rock concert. Every treasure sale participant received one parking space to hawk their wares, but some families brought so much stuff—umm . . . I mean treasure—that they needed two spaces. Everyone chipped in, got organized, and worked together for the coming onslaught of early morning deal-makers.

By sunrise, we were thanking God for a beautiful clear day. One group of teenagers found a creative way to capitalize on their Kingdom Assignment challenge. They put their minds and hearts together by organizing a bake night at their house and selling the scrumptious cookies and brownies to the sugar-deprived buyers and sellers. Working the stoves and coffee machines, these young people poured steaming cups of coffee and hot chocolate to help take the bite off the early morning chill as families eagerly awaited that first big sale. By day's end, the teenagers had raised over $200 for the poor and warmed many bellies.

By the time the buying and selling got started, almost seventy families had filled their parking spaces with assorted amounts of things once treasured. Hanging on racks and lying on old blankets were $125 Tommy Hilfiger sweaters that were now going for a buck. That must-have infomercial Ab-Roller, paid for in three easy installments, was now selling for $5.00, with the Ginzu knifes thrown in for free. The New Year's resolution stationary bike, which became a convenient clothes rack by March 1, was now peddled for $25. Compact discs so worth the listening at one time but now an embarrassment to even say we collected went for a quarter.

Strolling the Treasure Sale aisles, savvy shoppers picked, gawked, and sized up their prospective purchase looking for the diamond-in-the-rough. A party atmosphere filled the air as deals were made and friendships forged. By all the smiles and gleaming eyes, we knew the shoppers found good pickings and were not to be disappointed. Rugs. Mini bikes. Lamps. Napkin rings. Straw hats. Surfboards. Old computers. Jewelry. Hawaiian memorabilia. Books. Silk flower arrangements. Big Wheels. Dishes.

Lots of clothing. Towels. Coffee mugs. Televisions. Tables. Baskets. Beds.

From taking the time to go through their treasure, waking up early, and setting up their selling space, to wheeling and dealing—every Kingdom Assignment participant demonstrated the first sign that we have found leads to a life of significance. That sign is the *transforming power of sacrifice*.

## The Significance of Sacrifice

Some of you might be thinking these people just gave away stuff they needed to get rid of anyway. That's true, but the treasure sale cost them more than you might think. How many people do you know that are willing to go through their belongings, separate the junk from the

THE FIRST
SIGN OF
SIGNIFICANCE:

*sacrifice*

jewels, box it all up, pack it in the car, pay an entry fee for advertising, and then spend the rest of their Saturday selling items they receive no personal profit from, when instead they could be sitting on the couch watching their favorite Pac–10 team?

To live a life of significance, you must be willing
to sacrifice.
Sacrifice costs.
If it doesn't cost anything, you have to ask
yourself, is it really sacrifice?

*Sacrifice* is the first sign of significance. Sacrifice is the
practice of giving up something you treasure, something
that costs you personally, for a higher cause. The motivation for this kind of giving is not guilt but love.

We sometimes give for the wrong reasons, which
focuses our giving back on us. It's not uncommon for
people who have been blessed by God to wonder why
God has blessed them and not others. Instead of our giving flowing naturally out of our gratefulness, we become
motivated by guilt rather than love. Our giving, then, is
trying to relieve an internal tension. True sacrifice is motivated by love, and this love is focused on what our choices
and sacrifices can do for someone else.

When God's people desire to make a true sacrifice to
His glory, to the benefit of others, and for their own joy,
stories follow.

## The Eye of the Beholder

As I browsed the aisles of the treasure sale, passing by
each family's space and lingering around to see if anything would catch my eye, I must admit that most of the
"treasure" was the same sort of dented, dusty, worn-out
items that fill my closets and garage shelving. Things that
were valuable at one time. You know, those must-have

items seen in shopping malls, outlet centers, on television, or surfing online. Stuff we had to have at the time but now couldn't wait to get rid of. Many participants used the Treasure Sale as an opportunity to do a little early spring cleaning. Nothing wrong with that. Every Saturday our intersections are lined with garage and moving sale signs, but that money goes into the pocket of whoever's doing the sale. This was different because the Treasure Sale money was going directly into somebody else's pocket. Most of the Treasure Sale participants had the goal of raising at least $100 for the poor. Anything over the top was gravy for the cause. What I didn't see, however, were many high-ticket items . . . items that were truly worth a lot of money.

That is, until I met Sharon.

As I approached a small folding table, before me lay an exquisite display of fine Waterford Crystal, Lladro Statues, and Faberge Eggs. These were expensive, beautiful items usually found in expensive boutiques and exclusive stores, not a church garage sale . . . oops! I mean Treasure Sale. Curious, I began to pry for answers.

"Why such expensive items?" I asked.

I'll never forget Sharon's response.

Standing next to her table, Sharon told me that every single thing she owns is on loan from God. Picking up a small delicate statue to illustrate her point, Sharon looked at me and said, "It's not mine; it's His. To give back junk to my King would be an insult. So, I chose the better things to sell in order to give to God my best effort.

My relationship with God is my most important possession and treasure!"

## Stubborn Faith

Rob is a healthy, active, Orange County, American male. How do I know? He loves motorcycles. I don't run into many men out this way west that don't either own a motorcycle or wish their wives would let them have one. It's the modern horse every guy wants, but on weekends when many a guy is driving the kids around town in the minivan, what he's really doing at the stoplight is daydreaming about cruising on a dual exhaust, leather-strapped, chrome-plated Harley hog.

Like many of the possessions we own, Rob's motorcycle had a lot of fond memories attached to it. On weekends, Rob traveled with his friends along the southern California coast and on the long, twisting local mountain roads. He took his kids out and taught them the love of riding.

So, when Rob attended church and heard about the idea of selling a possession for the poor, the one thought that came to the forefront of his mind was his beloved motorcycle.

"This one might hurt," Rob thought. "My bike would be the last thing on my list of things to sell. It's my baby. My prized possession."

But God was tugging on his heart.

Rob's one thing could do a lot of good for a whole lot of people.

When he told Julie, his wife, about the dilemma he was facing, she reminded him, "It's just a motorcycle!"

Rob decided to do the math. He knew he could sell it for over $5,000 and that money could help a lot of poor families in our area. It wasn't long before Rob put an ad in the local paper to sell his treasured bike.

Two months later, Rob slipped an envelope containing a check for $5,600 in the basket for the Thanksgiving Kingdom Assignment offering. His treasured motorcycle was out of his garage and now taking up storage space in heaven. He no longer cruises the great American highways, but he is well on his way to a life of significance.

## One Woman's Trash Is Another Man's Treasure

Bruce is Kristin's husband. Like a lot of guys, even Christian guys, Bruce went to church, but his attendance usually came with a nudge from Kristin. Sure, he was a believer, but there were a lot of other things he could be doing on a sunny California Sunday. Bruce had a passion for activities like surfing, snowboarding, and skateboarding with his pals.

On the morning of Kingdom Assignment 2 during the 8:00 A.M. service, Kristin was bouncing her newborn baby in the church foyer. Bruce sat by himself in the front of the auditorium when Denny gave the Kingdom Assignment 2 challenge. When Kristin watched Bruce get out of his seat, walk up to the front, and drop his "Count

Me In" card into the basket, not only was she surprised, she hoped against hope that her husband was considering selling the same thing she had in mind: their classic '68 Cadillac convertible that took up a ton of room in their garage.

Kristin thought, "Ahha! Now I can get my space back!" Kristin's main reason for getting rid of the Caddy was so she, like most of us, could have more space to store more stuff. She breathed a sigh of relief, knowing she was going to get that monstrosity out of her garage.

As he dropped his name in the basket, Bruce was thinking the exact opposite. Bruce was actually thinking about all the junk Kristin had in the house—and what perfect timing it was for it to go.

*He thought, she thought.*

But God had different plans.

After sharing their ideas with each other about it on the way home, they were at a standstill. As they pulled into their driveway at home and popped open the garage door, Bruce saw something that caught his attention. Tucked away behind the '68 Cadillac was a garage full of hidden treasures Bruce had forgotten about. In the snowboard industry in which he works, Bruce was given countless product samples of snowboards, ski boots, powder pants, and other assorted gear. Way more stuff than he could ever need or use. Bruce knew our high school ministry was going to be taking their annual ski trip in a few months, and there were plenty of students who couldn't afford the high cost of snowboard equipment and clothes. Why not hold a snowboard gear sale for all the high school students and sell it all off for real cheap?

Bruce realized this was a win-win opportunity for kids and Kingdom Assignment 2. So, for the next few weekends, Bruce found every opportunity he could to sell his snowboard gear. The students were able to get a bargain on equipment and Bruce met his goal of giving $1000 for the poor.

But that's not all.

As Bruce sold his equipment, God began to work on his heart. Not only did Bruce have a renewed desire for a significant relationship with God, he also began to take an interest in our high school ministry. What if God could use him to help today's young people? Bruce met with our high school pastor and began serving as a leader in the youth ministry. Bruce initially thought he'd just be selling off a bunch of excess snowboard gear. Now he has a place of ministry, watching and helping teenagers step closer to Christ in the Kingdom.

And Kristin? Well, she's a happy camper. Even though that Cadillac is still taking up space in their garage, she has a husband who has a passion for God and who is excited to go to church on Sunday. To her, that's what it's all about.

## The Spirit of Sacrifice

One of the best examples in Scripture that reflects this significant spirit of sacrifice is found in Paul's second letter to the Corinthians. The situation in the early church was one of great persecution, such that some of the believers were extremely hard-pressed financially. Paul used this occasion to write to the Christians in the Greek city of Corinth. As an example, he spoke of the sacrificial giving of the Macedonian church, who were concerned for their fellow brothers and sisters in Christ. Paul writes:

> And now, brothers, we want you to know about the grace that God has given the Macedonian churches. Out of the most severe trial, their overflowing joy and their extreme poverty welled up in rich generosity. For I testify that they gave as much as they were able, and even beyond their ability. Entirely on their own, they urgently pleaded with us for the privilege of sharing in this service to the saints. (2 Cor. 8: 1–4)

The Macedonian Christians demonstrated both the attitude and action of sacrificial giving, which was the evidence of the grace of God at work in their lives. The mark of sacrifice in our lives is not how much we give but how much it may have cost us, in some way, to let it go. Sacrifice is like that. It often means more to us than anyone else. Maybe that's why Paul said when the Macedonians gave sacrificially, the amount of their gifts was far exceeded by the overwhelming joy they received in doing so. Jesus noted that it wasn't the abundance of the Pharisees' gifts to the poor that were significant but rather the widow's mite, her penny, that was significant because what she gave was all she had.

Several weeks after hearing Kristin and Bruce's story, we heard the story behind the story. After selling the snowboard ski equipment in their garage and giving over $1000 to Kingdom Assignment 2, what we didn't know was that they had been living off their savings for the last two years as Bruce tried to start a new business. He had left the successful sunglass company where he worked as vice-president, feeling this was an important decision to the life of his family. Kristin told us that after the $1000 was collected, Bruce put the cash in an envelope and put it in a safe place until Thanksgiving weekend. Money was tight that week, so tight they didn't have enough money to buy a gallon of milk at the grocery store. Kristin was eyeing the Kingdom Assignment 2 money. What would it hurt, she thought, to just sneak a five and try and replace it later?

But she resisted, got in the car with the kids, and decided to dig as much change as she could out of the car ashtray. When she got to the store, she still didn't have enough. Instead of turning back home and checking between the seat cushions of the living room couch, she checked her wallet one last time. There it was! She didn't know how it got there, but there was a crisp $20 bill just sitting there. To this day she has no idea where the money came from. She is convinced God put it there to teach her a grand lesson in faith she will never forget, that when you are obedient, God will always be faithful.

Bottom line: Kristin and Bruce could have easily kept a few dollars for themselves, and no one would have known; but instead they willingly and joyfully gave the money to the poor as they trusted God to meet their needs.

Significance always follows sacrifice, but before we sacrifice what we treasure for a greater good, we might be asked to surrender the unexpected.

CHAPTER 3

# *Letting Go*

I'm like a lot of moms in America. I love my kids and I like to shop for them.

In case you're wondering, just because I am a minister's wife doesn't mean I can't still get caught up in the same crazes everyone else does. So, although I am embarrassed to say this, in the past few years I've acquired a large collection of Ty Beanie Babies. You know—those cute, fit-in-the-palm-of-your-hand, furry fabric toys filled with beans.

It all started innocently enough. As word got out about Beanie Babies, I picked up one here and one there for my kids. Soon, however, I stepped into the Beanie Baby bear trap . . . and I was hooked, but not for my kids—*myself*. As friends and family walked into the guest room of our home, they were assaulted by a vast barrage of multicolored stuffed animals. It'd be too strong to say it was a shrine, although others might have found that word accurate.

I could probably write a book on my Beanie Baby adventures, but let me share with you just a few. Bear with me.

For our twenty-fifth wedding anniversary, Denny and I took a long-awaited vacation traveling up the western coast during the height of the McDonald's Teenie Weenie Beanie craze. We stopped at virtually every McDonald's along the way so I could put my hands on the coveted collectibles. Of course, Mickey D's did not sell them all at once, so I had to be strategic in my stops. A new animal came out every few days, which was an insidious promotion plot to extend the mania. Like some of you, I was one of "those people" that stood in long lines and bought happy meals just for the TWBs. Pathetic, isn't it?

Soon, just the smell of McDonald's French fries made me nauseous. Focused on my furry friends, I'd order my Happy Meal, perform an animal rescue by taking my Teenie Beanie out of the bag, and hand the food to a nearby homeless person or starving college student. Denny knew I lost it when I began mapping out where in each city McDonald's was during our return drive home.

Or what about the time when we were on Catalina Island for my sister's wedding? My sister Jana and her fiancé, Rick Yost, had planned their wedding in the quaint, emerald-watered town of Avalon, but a few family members and I were in for a big surprise we hadn't planned. One day, Denny and I and my two nephews, Tyler and Britt, walked into a small boutique where we found the mother bear of all Ty bears, Princess.

Princess was the rare bear impossible to find on the mainland. She was so new, so royal, and so British, we knew we had scored something big. As we browsed the Beanie display, we tried to contain our enthusiasm for striking pay dirt. Like myself, Tyler and Britt were serious Beanie collectors, and we relished in our discovery. This was our secret, and the shopkeeper knew we were eager to get our hands on Princess. When we asked if she had more Princess bears for sale, in a lowered voice, she said, "I think I have one left. I was saving it for my son, but I'll sell it to you."

*Yes!!!*

I felt a little guilty, but not enough to stop her. She asked us to step outside the shop and in a few minutes, she brought out not one Princess bear, but one for each of us . . . as if this was a big drug deal going on. We discovered too that she had other rare or retired Beanie Babies, so every day we found convenient reasons to return to her store.

On the last day of our trip, we all started comparing notes. We realized she had sold us seventy Beanie Babies! I think we paid more in Beanie Babies than we did in wedding gifts. And I think you can still read the word "sucker" on my forehead if you catch me in the right light.

One of my best Beanie Baby sources was a friend of mine who worked at a local bed-and-breakfast. Often, she would get a load in, and if I called at just the right time, I'd be able to snag a few at the $6.99 price. When you buy in bulk, price matters. One day I called my friend and discovered she just received a gold mine of new Beanies. I hopped in my car and tore over to the B & B. A bit excited, I drove a little too fast. Okay, I broke the speed limit. The kind police officer writing my ticket said I was going sixty-seven in a fifty-mph zone. Oops!

My new Beanie Baby cost $7.35.

My ticket and traffic school cost $189.40.

Don't they have support groups for these types of problems?

## Give It Up

When the idea came for Kingdom Assignment 2 that we were to sell something of sacrifice and bring the money to the church for the poor, I knew exactly what I needed to do. One morning, after praying about what part I was going to play in selling a possession for the poor, I sat up in bed and said, "I know what treasure God is wanting me to give up."

God's message to me was plain and simple: He was calling me to sell my Beanie Babies and give the money to the poor. I had been successful in attaining a complete set of these coveted creatures, but now God was calling me to do something significant with them.

And so, on the day of the Treasure Sale, I set up a table and displayed all one hundred and fifty retired and beautiful Beanie Babies. My intention was to sell everything together. I must say, it was an impressive display. My Beanies had never been touched by a sticky child's hand and the tags were in mint condition. That's Beanie

talk for the highest value of a hot commodity. My dream
was to sell the lot for $700 dollars. I prayed about it.
What was God going to show me? I questioned God,
"Lord, what miracle do You have in store here?"

My plan was to sell all to the highest bidder. I was
ready for a *successful* sale.

Like Bruce's Cadillac, God had a different plan.

I placed a sign in front of my table:

ALL BEANIES — SOLD TOGETHER — MAKE OFFER

At least fifty people came by my little space. They
ignored my sign and asked me, "How much for this
Beanie?" or "How much for that one?" I smiled to
myself thinking, *These people don't get it*, as I slowly
peeled the Beanie out of their hand, saying, "I'm selling
them all together if you would like to make a bid."

I got many strange looks that day.

The potential buyers could see the dollar signs in my
eyes, and they had no intention of giving in to a crazed
collector like myself.

Convinced the Beanie bidding was about to get hot,
real hot, I patiently awaited for my first bidder. A beautiful Hispanic woman dropped by my table. She was
pregnant, probably about seven months, and like so
many women soon to give birth, she had a glowing,
peaceful radiance about her. Next to the woman was her
small, dark-haired daughter, who looked about seven or
eight years old. She asked me in halting English how
much I wanted for my Beanie Baby collection.

"I'm taking best offer for the whole lot," I replied in my best sales voice. "What would you like to bid?" I waited to hear her response, hoping for my first bid.

"Hmm," she said. "I can offer you twenty dollars."

*Twenty dollars?*

Remember Jim Carey in *The Grinch Who Stole Christmas. . .*

*Oh! The audacity . . . the unmitigated gall!!*

Well, I didn't want to embarrass her by saying that twenty dollars for a hundred and fifty rare-'n'-retired Beanie Babies was the most ridiculous thing I'd ever heard, so instead I politely asked her for her name and phone number.

"I'll call you if that works out, Sandra," I said through a strained smile, knowing darn well I had no intention of selling *my collection* for such a small amount. *Twenty bucks? I might as well give 'em away.*

As the other buyers and sellers were doing deals all around me, to my dismay, no one showed any interest in buying my Beanie Baby collection.

*Okay, Lord, so where's the miracle?*

Discouraged, I loaded all one hundred and fifty Beanies back into my car. You can sell them on e-Bay, I told myself. Other sellers tried to console me, "Don't worry. You'll have tons of bidders on e-Bay." But I didn't want to sell them on e-Bay.

When I arrived home, Denny helped me put my collection back in the guest room. I was miserable. I was grumbling that I had not accomplished *my mission*, and

I couldn't get over the ridiculously low bid that woman made. She must have some sort of faith because her $20 bid was crazy. I knew it and she knew it.

But then, within a few hours, God began to show me *His mission*.

As I stewed in my unsuccessful sales attempt, a Scripture came to me: "You do not have, because you do not ask God" (James 4:2). Even though the bid was so ridiculously low, Sandra had the faith to ask. Now it was my turn to have the faith to respond. I got out the paper that Sandra had written her number on, picked up the phone, and dialed her number. A young child answered.

"Is Sandra there?" I asked.

The child said yes and went to get her mom.

"Hi, Sandra, my name is Leesa, and you made an offer of $20 for the Beanie Babies."

"Yes."

"Well, then, you're the highest bidder for my Beanies. You can have them for $20."

On the other end of the line I heard something like a giggle, a gasp, and a joyous scream all at the same time. I then heard her speak to her eight-year-old daughter in Spanish, who came on the line. "My mom asked me to give you directions to our house," she said.

As it turned out, Sandra lived just a few miles away. Within minutes, I drove to her home to find Sandra standing out in front. I wasn't sure if she was too embarrassed to show me her house—or perhaps she had just sneaked $20 from her husband's wallet and didn't want him to find out.

Though it wasn't even Thanksgiving yet, with a big smile I said, "Merry Christmas."

Sandra had an even bigger smile on her face, one that I'll never forget. "Thank you," she said, as she pushed a crumpled bill into my hand.

Her eight-year-old daughter came out and by the look on her face, I don't think I've ever seen two happier people in my whole life. I knew in that moment that I had done something significant, quite possibly one of the most significant things I've ever done in my life. I had given Sandra something she could have never afforded, and I received something all the money or Beanie Babies in the world could have never afforded me.

"Let's take 'em inside," I said, as I helped Sandra and her daughter carry the boxes of Beanie Babies into their home.

Those boxes never felt lighter.

## Sweet Surrender

On our refrigerator, we have a magnet picture frame that reads around the edges, "Let go and let God." Over the years, it has held the pictures of our daughters, Brooke and Natalie, with their current boyfriends. It's been a constant reminder to them and to us not to hold on to their relationships too tightly and to remember that God needs to be in control of every aspect of their lives.

Now that Brooke and Natalie are both married to wonderful, godly men, I still keep a picture of the two couples tucked under the frame. Everyone in the Bellesi family knows that to "Let go and let God" is not a one-time lesson but a lifetime goal. It's a lesson of surrender we all need to be reminded of every so often.

*Surrender*—the second sign of significance—is the practice of daily committing all of who you are and all that you own to the Lord. Surrender means giving up whatever treasure is keeping you from a significant relationship with God. It is the daily practice of relinquishing whatever you hold near and dear to the rule and reign of Jesus Christ. Depending on your particular circumstances, surrender may mean different things to you at different times in your life, but it always involves a degree of giving up and giving in to the Lord. Therein lies the difficulty of surrendering . . . giving up and giving in to God what we so often treasure for ourselves. Sometimes, that difficulty is not so much parting with what we have but parting with what we want, what we expect, what we feel we need or deserve.

THE SECOND SIGN OF SIGNIFICANCE:

*surrender*

When Kingdom Assignment 2 was started, it didn't sound too difficult, particularly since we had a specific goal in mind of helping the poor. Out of a thousand people who signed up for the assignment, I'm sure several took it as an altruistic opportunity to do some early spring cleaning for a noteworthy cause. But many took it much more seriously than that. Some saw it as a call from the Lord to part with some stuff that, in some conscious or unconscious way, actually stood between them and the Lord. Like RYR, beneath the surface of this seemingly simple assignment, God was working to bring to light some things hidden in their hearts. And like Kingdom Assignment 1, God was using this assignment to show people that it had as much to do with them as it did with the poor who were the beneficiaries of all the proceeds. In many ways, this assignment was *more* about the givers and *less* about the receivers. It was about each person's willingness to look into his or her heart and surrender whatever it was that each one was hanging on to.

When I was challenged to give away my Beanie Babies, this was a form of surrender I hadn't experienced before. I knew there was a lesson to be learned, but I was not expecting to learn it this way. Sandra didn't know that what I held in those boxes was estimated at about $1,500 or more, but I didn't know that I was going to give all the Beanies away for $20. Put another way, I was as dumbfounded as Sandra. I had my expectation of how I wanted to sell my furry friends and how much I wanted to earn to give to the poor, but God had another plan for what He was asking me to do. The day I gave away my Beanies, I'm convinced that I received far more than Sandra and her daughter ever received.

I'll always wonder if Sandra knew the true value of what she held in those boxes—but then again, it doesn't matter. What was most important was asking myself whether I was willing to surrender what God was asking me to do for His glory and for His purpose.

## The Rest of the Story

One of the interesting features of the Lord's encounter with RYR is that Jesus never details for this man just how much his "donation" to the poor would help its recipients. For RYR, the real story and challenge are not how much he could help the poor by selling everything he owned, but rather in how much selling would truly benefit this young man to surrender what was keeping him from a significant relationship with God.

I'm reminded of the story of Jim Eliot, who was killed in the 1950s in the effort of bringing the gospel to the Auca Indians. In response to comments that he was a fool to risk his life to share Christ with a tribe of known headhunters, Eliot often said, *"He is no fool, who gives up what he cannot keep to gain what he cannot lose."* Those words have often rung in my ears. Jim Eliot knew and understood the value of surrender, the willingness to surrender his own life for the sake of something he valued even more, the Kingdom of God.

Most of us will never be asked to give our lives for the sake of Christ the way Jim Eliot did. Still, as believers, all of us are called to *live* every day for the sake of Christ. To live this way involves surrender. I probably don't need to tell you, but surrender is hard. Jesus reminds us in his encounter with RYR that it is *hard* for a rich man or woman to enter the Kingdom of God. In fact, Jesus said, it's easier for a "camel to go through the eye of a needle, than for a rich man to enter the kingdom of God." In short, he said, it's *impossible* on our own terms!

Yet, the truth is, our God deals in making the impossible possible—an ongoing reality in the lives of those who dare to surrender, of those who give up and give in to Him. When Jesus' disciples let it be known that they had given up *everything* to follow him, Jesus reassured them, "I tell you the truth, no one who has left home or wife or brothers or parents or children for the sake of the kingdom of God will fail to receive many times as much in this age and, in the age to come, eternal life" (Luke 18:29–30).

This is the kind of life Jesus lived . . . and this is the kind of life Jesus promises could be ours as well. I've discovered what it means to enjoy a life of significance in Christ, but for Denny, it began with a surrender of the heart at a time when he knew God was asking him to give something up in order to go further.

## A Surrender of the Heart

When I graduated from Grant High School in North Hollywood, California, I was a Christian and a leader in my church's youth group. I was also a pretty good basketball player, good enough to play college ball.

In the fall of 1969, I enrolled at San Diego State, which was a time when freshmen were not allowed to play varsity sports. Although I only got to play on the freshmen team, I didn't care. I loved playing hoops, and playing for a Division I school made it all the better. I stood 5'9" tall in my white Converse canvas sneakers and didn't stand a chance of dominating the game, so I knew I wasn't going to be a star and desperately wanted to fit in. Since I had three blue-chip recruits ahead of me on the depth chart, I had to hustle on defense and prove to the coach that this 5'9" white guy had something to contribute. During tryouts, I shot the lights out and made my way onto the team.

After fitting in by making the team, there's another thing I did to fit in: I laid low in my Christian faith, keeping silent about the fact that I was a follower of Christ. This was my first time away from home, and I wanted to see what the college wild life was all about. I didn't hook up with a campus ministry. I didn't go to church. And I certainly didn't carry my Bible to basketball practice.

For me, this was totally out of character. Between high school graduation and the start of college, I had been totally involved with our church's high school group at church, where I worked as a summer intern. Before school started in the fall at San Diego State, I received a phone call from the San Diego director of Youth for Christ, a youth ministry organization. The director asked me to look him up when I arrived on campus and mentioned that he was interested in my working with youth in San Diego. I said I would, but once classes began, I made no effort to contact him.

Meanwhile, I was a third-string player, sitting on the bench and watching a lot of basketball. On one road trip, the team went to the University of California at Santa Barbara, which was also known for its stellar reputation as one of the great party schools in the country. We lost a game we should have won, which infuriated our coach. From what I saw from the team's performance, the players didn't care, and the coach was probably right. We were spending the night in Santa Barbara, and everyone knew what that meant. The game was over and the team couldn't wait for the party to begin.

After showering and leaving the lockers, we collected our per diem meal money. Except for the players hooking up with the local girls back in their hotel rooms, I watched teammate after teammate walking toward the liquor store to buy vodka and orange juice.

I was invited to join them, but I made some excuse and headed back to my room, feeling very unhappy and unsatisfied where I was at in this stage of my life. I knew I was running away from God. I knew I should be on a different team at San Diego State—the team trying to do something significant for Christ.

The next day, after all the partying was over, we boarded the bus home. While sitting on the bus and reflecting on how unhappy I was, I heard a little voice say to me, *"Is this how you really want to spend the rest of your college years?"*

Deep inside, I knew the answer to that question. I felt compelled to leave the team, but I had never quit anything in my life. Playing collegiate basketball had been a lifelong dream of mine . . . and dreams die hard.

Despite the ambivalent feelings, I knew the Lord was asking me to sell all that I owned at that point in my

life—my basketball career. I knew what I had to do. I
may have not been the RYR, the Shaq or Tiger Woods of
my time, but there was something standing between me
and the Lord. It was time for me to make a choice for
significance over limited, short-term basketball success.

The next day, I made an appointment to see my
coach. After listening to me explain my decision to vol-
untarily end my basketball career, my coach looked me
in the eyes and said, "If you quit this team, you'll be a
quitter all your life."

That's a pretty intimidating statement for an eighteen-
year-old sitting in the office of a college basketball coach.
With a resolve I didn't quite understand at the time, I
looked back at my coach and said, "I have never quit
anything before in my life, but I really feel there is something else more important that I need to be doing."

With that, I excused myself, hopped into my car, and
drove over to the San Diego Youth for Christ office
located nearby. When I walked in, the director whom I
had spoken with earlier that summer, looked up and said,
"I was praying for you this morning."

I told him my story about the Santa Barbara road trip
and quitting the State basketball team. He looked
intrigued and after a few minutes spoke up. "Tell you
what. We have a staff meeting in ten minutes. Can you
join us? I'm sure we can find something for you to do
around here."

Leaving the basketball team, my "one thing" during
my college years, was the start of more than thirty

wonderful years in ministry. It happened because I was willing to surrender something very close to me—my days as a gym devotee and basketball jock—for whatever God had waiting for me. It's a decision I struggled with, but once I let go, once I surrendered, I never looked back.

# CHAPTER 4

# Riding the Wave of Significance

At twenty-six years old, Hyatt Moore had achieved everything he had dreamt about since he was a young boy. Growing up on Southern California beaches, Hyatt dreamed of having a job using his abilities in graphic design. In his early twenties, without a completed college education, he was hired as the art director at *Surfer Magazine*, the preeminent magazine of surf culture. Cropped close-ups of knobby kneed surfers, water skimming the tops of their heads, transformed readers' imaginations, placing them in exotic locations around the globe. His work, scheduled around the current wave conditions, enabled people to look at life from the inside of perfect barrels—the glossy pages offering endless waves and inviting water.

Hyatt had the most enviable job anyone could ever want. It was his responsibility to oversee the creative design of the magazine every month. His life was surfing, and he used his creative talents to design and inspire, working with the coolest people who understood that there was more to life than wearing a tie and punching a time clock.

Dream job. Beautiful wife. Silver Porsche. Fast boat.

What else could anyone ask for? He had everything he'd always wanted; but as he told us, *"Life was not complete."*

Like many people who have everything they ever dreamed of but feeling something is missing, like RYR, Hyatt went searching. And like many of his contemporaries in the 1960s, Hyatt's searching became a way of life. Like a late August swell on a hot summer day, he rode the waves of smoking pot and tripping on acid. But nothing seemed to fill the hole in his life, the hole in his heart. In his wanderings, Hyatt came upon a Christian book called *The Late Great Planet Earth*, by Hal Lindsey.

Hyatt began to read about his need for God, and it wasn't long before he was on his knees, confessing his sins and asking Jesus to be his Savior. For the next two years, Hyatt submersed himself in the Scriptures, learning what it meant to be a follower of Christ. He found a small group of men who mentored him, and he became involved in a local church.

As Hyatt grew in his relationship with God, he began to take a few evenings every week to drive to an open field near his home in Dana Point, California. In the green grass of the field overlooking the deep blue of the Pacific, Hyatt stood and prayed out loud. As he wrestled with what he was supposed to do with his life, many a conversation with God became argumentative.

"What is it you want from me, Lord? If I give my whole life to you, it will become boring, and I'll surely look like a loser to my peers and family."

Sitting behind his drawing table at *Surfer*, Hyatt knew he had success and prestige. And now his newfound relationship with God gave him the peace and satisfaction he was looking for. Since he openly shared his faith with his coworkers and friends, everyone knew where he stood. Still, Hyatt knew God wanted more from him . . . but what could it be?

One evening in the field, something happened to Hyatt. As he prayed, he spoke to God not with joy-filled emotion but with willful commitment. Convinced God was calling him to a life of obedience and not of comfort or convenience, he said out loud, "I will serve you with my life." Again, this was not a moment of happy, peaceful feelings; rather, Hyatt was ambivalent about it all. It was simply an act of obedience.

Convinced he was destined for a boring life, Hyatt said, "I figured, at best, I'd probably only live another sixty years. What could be worse? Living an uneventful life or spending eternity without reward?"

A month later, Hyatt was sitting in an evening church service waiting for God to tell him his next step. A young missionary woman, the guest speaker that day, was giving a passionate call for the people in the audience to consider going to the mission field. She worked with an organization called Wycliffe Bible Translators, a missionary organization whose goal is to translate the Bible into every dialect in the world. This young woman was challenging everyone to get out of his or her comfort zone because there was so much work to be done. Hyatt was impressed.

Hyatt and his wife, Anne, watched as the young missionary clicked through a series of slides showing the living conditions in the Third World country where she served. A slide came up of the mission's art department, which was nothing like Hyatt's desk at *Surfer*. Funny, Hyatt thought, it's just a desk and some rubber cement.

Hyatt felt his heart warm to the idea of going on the mission field. Who would have thought? He and Anne began to pray about it, and they soon became convinced this was where God was calling them. Once the decision was made, Hyatt wasn't bored . . . he was excited! He sold his Porsche and gave away his boat. He quit his job at *Surfer*. His fellow staff members wondered if he had lost his mind. Yes, Hyatt was doing something radical. If he ever thought God was going to give him a boring life, he was wrong. His life took on a new significance of great proportion.

When Hyatt, Anne, and their children left for the mission field, that wide-eyed missionary novice, inexperienced in the languages and the customs of the small countries in which they stayed, went on to become the United States president of Wycliffe Bible Translators— an organization that today has a worldwide staff of six thousand. They have completed the Bible in over five hundred languages and are working on a thousand beyond that. Awarded by the United Nations, today Wycliff is the largest literacy program in the world, giving men, women, and children opportunities they would never have had.

God even gave Hyatt his original job back. *Surfer Magazine* hired him again years later—doing mission's work by day and working at *Surfer* by night, paying him a full-time salary for part-time work.

Hyatt has now traveled the globe many times over. Like you and me, God isn't finished with him yet. A few years ago, he purchased a small paint set and began to teach himself how to paint. He began painting the faces of the local people he met in foreign countries in his travels across the world. People that are in the far ends of the earth. People that live in places you and I could only dream of seeing. In a short time, Hyatt became a proficient painter and began displaying his art.

One evening, Hyatt displayed his art during one of our church services. As he spoke to the congregation (much like the young missionary he had listened to years earlier), he displayed a twenty-by-five-foot replica of the Last Supper, but it wasn't Da Vinci's classic. Using strong, bold colors, Hyatt used the same Da Vinci Last Supper layout, but the disciples around the table took on a new look. Surrounding Jesus *were the faces of* men from South America. Men from Africa. Men from Papua New Guinea. Men from Asia. It was a glorious sight as people of all color found their place at the table.

## The Significance of Submission

Hyatt could have ignored God's calling. He could easily have shut it out and made excuses for what he really heard God calling him to be and do. Oh, but what a life he would have missed! Hyatt and Anne Moore now travel the world, telling their stories of faith and displaying Hyatt's art. Hyatt's *one thing* was his life, his direction, his focus. That may seem like a lot of "things" to you, but not to him. Hyatt felt he had to say "yes" to

THE THIRD SIGN OF SIGNIFICANCE:

*submission*

God with all of who he was. He had to do it in one lump sum, which was different from the day he asked Jesus for forgiveness.

When Hyatt gave his heart to Christ, that was acknowledging his need for a Savior. But in being a Christ follower, he realized he

needed to give everything of himself to God because everything he was and had belonged to God. Until he took the willful act of doing just that, he knew he was never going to live a life of true significance.

For followers of Jesus Christ, *submission* is the third sign of significance. Simply stated, submission is the practice of responding to the initiative of God's agenda and direction over our own. Submission is the heartbeat of Jesus' agonizing prayer in the Garden of Gethsemane: "Not my will, but Yours be done."

Unlike sacrifice and surrender, which can be one-time events, submission distinguishes itself as an ongoing lifestyle of personal obedience. Submission is about relinquishing our own and often-treasured will to the perspective and direction of God's greater will. Submission is trusting that God's way is better than our way and believing that He has our best intentions in mind. The truth of the matter is God doesn't want our stuff as much as He wants our heart.

Submission settles the matter of who or what is going to have first dibs on your heart, and then choosing to obey and live accordingly. In the Gospels, when Jesus confronted men and women about following Him, He always zeroed in on the stuff that made them tick. That's why Jesus' method of calling men and women to follow him is unique and different for every person He meets. Jesus starts with people where *they* are and deals with *their* issue, the *one thing* that has a grip on their heart, because He knows that until that one thing is dealt with, they can't or won't come and *truly* follow Him.

Read through the Gospels and see how Jesus was always able to identify the one thing in the heart of every person He met.

- For the woman at the well in Samaria, her one thing was her secret living arrangement with a man, who was just one in a long list of other men. (John 4)
- For Zacchaeus, his one thing was his unscrupulous character as a tax collector. (Luke 19)
- For the woman caught in adultery, her one thing was her secret sin and shame. (John 8)

- For the man lying at the pool of Bethesda, it was whether he wanted to get well. (John 5)
- For Nicodemus the lawyer, it was his personal and religious pride. (John 3)
- For the first disciples, it was the security of their livelihood. (Luke 5)
- For Saul on the road to Damascus, it was his anger and arrogance. (Acts 9)
- For RYR, it was his money and possessions. (Luke 18)

As we stated at the beginning of this book, everyone has *one thing*. It can be different at different seasons of our lives, but when asked, some people immediately know what it is. What's yours? Only in identifying our *one thing* and submitting our whole selves to the good and perfect will of God can we ever hope to experience a life of significance. And if you've ever wrestled with submitting to the will of God, rest assured, you are not alone.

## Trisha's Story

In 1987, when Coast Hills was just getting started, Trish Van Mourick began attending with her family. Soon after, she became a believer in Jesus Christ. Leesa and I saw tremendous potential in Trish. She had a great heart for God, capable skills, and inspirational leadership ability. A few years later after growing in her relationship with God, she was just the person we needed to develop a MOPS (Mothers of Preschoolers) ministry at the church.

Because she had a couple preschoolers of her own, she worked only part-time leading MOPS. But as I saw her leadership skills grow while she breathed life into new MOPS groups, I knew she was one special person.

In 1992, I asked Trish if she would come on board as the Director of Women's Ministry at Coast Hills. She told me that she felt ill-equipped for the task, but I knew she would be perfect to build a strong women's ministry in a fast-growing church. By this time, Trish had three children, and she was someone who managed to be in two places at once. Willing to look past any personal limitations, Trish took the position we offered and, within a short time, rallied a team of women to develop it into a thriving ministry for women to connect and grow together in Christ.

But after five years of leading the women's ministry, Trish sensed a new sort of Kingdom Assignment. Her three children were growing, and she had an increased desire to be home with them before they grew up and left. Like many career women, Trish wrestled with the pull of professional life and home life.

About the same time Trish was considering leaving her position at Coast Hills, Steve Arterburn, author and radio host of *New Life Live*, approached her about becoming the executive director of *Women of Faith*, a large, national conference ministry. For over twenty-five weekends a year, *Women of Faith* fills 15,000-seat arenas from Seattle to Miami with one-day conferences, offering women inspirational Bible teaching and worship. Word had gotten out about Trish's leadership and organizational talents. Now Steve was asking if she was interested in accepting the position.

In one sense, this was a dream come true for Trish. She loved the responsibility of overseeing large events, and she ran them well. She knew she was ready for the task and knew this was the career challenge of a lifetime. She was being handed the keys to the chance to lead a movement impacting more than 300,000 lives a year. It also provided an opportunity for meeting and strategizing with some of the most notable Christian leaders and speakers, a nice paycheck, and plenty of compliments for leading such a significant ministry. The job was prestigious and part of her said, "Ooh, this would be so great!"

But was that what God wanted for her? Was this God's best for her and her family? In her own words, Trish said, "I realized that God was taking me on a helicopter ride to look at my life. God gave me a picture of where I could go with this new position, but He was also giving me a chance to see what was really important in my life. I felt the Lord was saying, 'Yes, you are ready for this . . . but look at the cost.' My career to this point had not been an obstacle, but the moment God called me to this crossroads, it became one. I knew what I had to do. It was the only way for me to be truly happy and know I was in the center of God's will, which was my strongest desire."

Trish was, of course, flattered in being asked to lead *Women of Faith*, and she struggled with saying no, but that's exactly what she did. In fact, she was so sure God was calling her to something higher that she came to me and told me she needed to leave her position at Coast Hills. Nothing could detour her. She was on a mission to do what God was calling her to do, and nothing could change her mind.

Her words were simple, "Denny, my family needs me."

What could I say to that? She was a busy mom to an eighth grader, a sixth grader, and a third grader, so I knew she was making a choice that was right for her and that honored God.

It's been a few years since Trish has taken on this new role as a full-time mom, but she loves it. She now has three teenagers and feels her children need her more than they ever have. I recently talked with her daughter Emily to get her perspective on her mom's career move. Here is what Emily, a sophomore in high school, said: "I love when I come home from school and my mom asks me how my day was. She really has time to listen. She's not stressed, running around and giving me distracted attention. She gives me her full attention. I know my other friends don't have that, and I can't live without it."

Emily knows significance when she sees it.

Trish told me, "Turning down the executive director position and my work at the church has been worth every loss that the world may say it was, because what I have gained far surpasses all the material success this earth can bring."

In submitting herself to God's call on her life, Trish recommends that moms who have the choice (for financial reasons, most single moms don't have this choice) seriously ponder whether to leave a career to raise children at home and ask themselves: *Who and what am I listening to? Today's culture or Christ? What is the driving motivation of my life? Is it my career? To have the perfect party, the perfect home, the perfect outfit? What is my most important ministry right now? What are my priorities?*

Trish wrapped her story and life experience up best by saying, "This doesn't mean that women forfeit all expression of their gifts, talents, service, or career. But there is a season for everything, and God is faithful to make it clear when and where it is."

## Buried Treasure

Submission has to do with obeying God's Word and trusting Him with the things closest to us. For some people, the most painful submission involves giving up the fears and secrets that no one else sees. The fears and secrets only God sees. Maybe you can relate to Trish's story, or maybe you will find the following stories hit home for you. They are stories that remind us that sometime it's not just worldly possessions or things that we carry around in the trunks of our cars or our purses that can stand between us and a significant relationship with God. It may be the stuff we carry buried deep within our hearts.

### Ted's Story

Ted was raised in a house divided. He had a Jewish father and a Protestant mother. His parents took a practical approach toward religious training, so they decided that Ted and his siblings would go to Hebrew school for three hours a day and Protestant class for three hours a day. Ted grew up confused and angry.

By the time he was in his late twenties, Ted was well on his way to a successful life. But he wanted nothing to do with organized religion. He had become a lawyer, operated chains of health clubs, and was the top salesman at any job he tried. He was also a talented musician working nights in clubs . . . a true renaissance man.

Sharp and good looking, on the outside Ted seemed confident. Little did anyone know that Ted struggled with fear. From the time he was a small child, fear and worry had controlled every aspect of his life. Many of the decisions he made on a daily basis surrounded his protective patterns of fear. Having always been in excellent physical health, Ted became acutely ill in 1990 with a seriously debilitating disease called Chronic Fatigue Syndrome. Back then it was called the Yuppie Flu, and Ted fit the category to a T. He was bedridden for several years and nearly lost all economic status he had worked so hard to achieve. Since the illness was considered incurable, fear and doubt plagued him as he worried whether he would ever recover.

Because of his medical condition, Ted had stopped dating. In 1994, his life was about to change when a friend set him up on a blind date. Her name was Cheri. She was cute and talented, and there was an immediate attraction between the two. During conversation that evening, Ted told Cheri that he had had an unusual religious upbringing. But when Ted asked her for a second date, Cheri wanted to make something clear to him. She had decided long ago that she would not have a second date with anyone who was not a follower of Jesus Christ.

Though Ted knew that his relationship with God was virtually nonexistent, he was convinced Cheri was a gift from Him. He wanted to marry her on the spot, but Cheri suggested he might want to meet her father first, who had been a pastor for over thirty years. Ted agreed to go to church with her. God had prepared his heart. After hearing the gospel, Ted stepped across the line into a new relationship with Christ. Within a few short years, Ted and Cheri grew in their faith together, became engaged, married, and started a family.

Ted pursued his passion for music and eventually became the worship leader at a church in his newfound hometown in Colorado. He was so talented that he was quickly put before a thousand people to lead worship. But being a new Christian, he had never taken the time to really know God's Word and His teachings. Even though Ted was following God's laws, like RYR, he discovered he had something from his past that was holding him back from becoming all that God desired for him to be. Ted's one thing was fear.

When Ted came into a relationship with Christ, the fear that contributed to his chronic fatigue syndrome didn't just go away; it only subsided. Ted prayed, but he didn't know how to protect his mind from his debilitating anxiety.

After several years of leading worship, feeling physically better and having a successful ministry experience, Ted's fears caught up with him. The chronic fatigue syndrome boomeranged back, making him ill and putting him out of work for almost a year. Unable to leave home, Ted prayed, *Lord, what are you trying to teach me?* He soon learned that God wanted to overcome his fears by renewing his mind. God pointed Ted to many relevant Scriptures related to fear and peace that gave him hope and direction. One of the most meaningful Scriptures he read was Psalm 119:71, "It was good for me to be afflicted so that I might learn your decrees."

As Ted read the Scriptures and confronted his fear, he learned to trust God with his life and let go of his future. The combination of listening, learning, and leaning on God during those ten months turned out to be the most productive time of his life because he finally began submitting his fears to God, choosing to walk by faith and not by sight. What seemed like a tragedy to Ted and his family became Ted's greatest gift. Today, Ted has a new lease on life. He wakes up enthusiastic every day, ready to face the world . . . not afraid anymore.

### Bonnie's Story

In the past year, America has been deluged with stories of secrets. The Enron financial scandal. The Catholic

Church's cover-up of child molestation. The FBI trying to hide potentially damaging information. We live in a society of inquiring minds, and it seems as if there's an insatiable desire for scandal. We have an incredible propensity for keeping secrets and exposing them. Secrets, like fears, can be the painful treasure we hold, keeping us from finding forgiveness and freedom and from moving on to living the life of significance God has designed us to live. If you've been keeping a secret treasure close to your heart, maybe you'll find a friend in Bonnie.

When Bonnie started high school in 1969, like most teenagers, she desperately wanted to fit in. She began sneaking out and going places she knew were off-limits. Before long she was out of control, experimenting with drugs, sex, and alcohol.

Her secret lifestyle began to cause problems at home, especially between her and her father. She blamed her parents for not understanding her and accused them of only worrying about what the neighbors thought.

At seventeen years old, Bonnie found herself pregnant and terrified. She'd always believed in God and knew that God created her, but she never thought it was important to get close to Him. "What am I going to do?" she screamed in her pillow one tearful night. She thought about her future. What about the prom, graduation, and college? She cried out to God, "How could you let this happen!" She pleaded with Him to make it all go away, wishing it were just a bad dream.

For weeks she refused to face the situation and naïvely tried to hide her secret. One day, her mother finally confronted her with what she suspected was the truth. They held each other and cried, but Bonnie's father was furious. He told her she was a disgrace to the family and an embarrassment to him. How could he face his friends and family?

Bonnie couldn't believe she was having a baby! Bonnie admitted that she didn't even like babysitting. This whole situation was an ugly mess, and she needed this mess to go away. So one afternoon, Bonnie made the mess go away by having an abortion. Not focusing on whether it was right or wrong, she felt abortion was the only realistic solution for her—and that's all that was important.

Into her adult life, Bonnie justified this choice for many years and buried all the hurt and anger that accompanied her secret decision. After all, it was her secret, and she told no one. She boldly moved on with her life. Or so she thought.

When Bonnie was asked if she would accompany her friend for an ultrasound to learn the sex of her friend's baby, Bonnie felt honored and thrilled to be invited. As the ultrasound began, her heart sank. For the first time she saw a life, a fetus. As she watched this real life flash across the screen, it was as if a ton of bricks landed on her head. Little did her friend know that the tears running down her cheeks were not tears of joy, but of grief and sadness. Bonnie tried to push God's subtle message away and sought to justify the choice she had made so many years ago. But keeping her secret was getting harder than she expected.

A few years after the ultrasound incident, a friend from work asked Bonnie if she'd like to attend church with her. After she ran out of excuses why she couldn't make it to church, Bonnie and her husband began to attend Coast Hills. One day, she prayed a simple prayer to ask Christ to come into her life. Bonnie felt herself growing in her faith and she knew she was forgiven for her sins. But there was still a place in her heart that was locked away, cold, dark, and full of anger. Bonnie knew it and God knew it.

There was a secret treasure between her and God.

Bonnie discovered that God had gifted her in the area of counseling, but in order to help others, she would first have to let herself be known. That meant being honest about her secret. Was she willing to give up her secret?

Then one day at a women's ministry meeting, Bonnie listened to the story of a woman who had gone through an abortion, became a Christian, and then started an abortion recovery ministry. Bonnie's heart began to pound. She thought to herself, *Maybe this is the opportunity for healing I've been praying for.*

Bonnie attended this women's recovery Bible study. Through its ministry, God took her on an incredible journey to many deep places she'd hidden inside for many years. Bonnie discovered just how big God's forgiveness really was not only for herself, but also in the forgiveness she extended to others. Bonnie would have missed an opportunity of significance if she hadn't been willing to speak the truth of her secret. Not only did coming forward with her secret help in her relationship with her husband, God also gave her the strength to begin repairing the relationship with her father, with whom she had not spoken in over seventeen years.

All this happened because Bonnie was willing to submit to God the treasured secret she had held on to so tightly. God used something that was so painful in Bonnie's life to give life to others also overwhelmed by the pain of a past decision.

- Are you in the middle of a difficult job choice?
- Is fear gripping you to the point of becoming paralyzing?
- Has a secret held you back from being all God has called you to be?

These "one things" take a submission of the heart. For Trish, Ted, and Bonnie, it brought about a change in lifestyle—a lifestyle that, when practiced, brings about a deeper significance than ever dreamed possible.

CHAPTER 5

# *Keeping It Simple*

Paul Gillis is a successful sales and marketing executive with a large national manufacturing company, but his passion lies in advancing God's Kingdom to the poor in a simple, yet significant way. Every month for the last eight years, Paul has led a team of volunteers from the mission's ministry in our church across the border into Mexico to help build homes for people who have no permanent place to live. Sometimes the group is small—maybe five to six people—and sometimes the group is as large as fifty people eager to make a difference for their brothers and sisters in Christ on the other side of the border.

That's what's beautiful about the simplicity of Paul's ministry. Not only does it look beyond the physical boundaries that so often separate people, but the ministry God has given him seeks to cross the economic and spiritual boundaries that exist even in the church. Paul's ministry teams are comprised of young and old alike, and every time he takes a group to Mexico, nobody comes back the same.

Through Paul's missionary journeys and our partnership with Amor Ministries, a Christian missions organization that works with local pastors and politicians in Tijuana, we have been able to build dozens of simple homes with families who previously slept in cardboard shacks. The key word here is "simple." The homes are basic, two-room, stucco structures with no plumbing, heating, or electricity. What makes our work (and many other churches' work) exciting is that we are building on foundations that have been laid by other colaborers in Christ.

Every spring, high school and college students from all over California gather to work with Amor to pour close to three hundred foundations in a two-week period for future homes. For the rest of the year, church and student groups come to this border town to finish the structures by framing, wrapping, and plastering the walls with two coats of hand-mixed stucco. A good team can usually finish one home in a couple of days! Because of the money raised by people selling treasured possessions in Kingdom Assignment 2, we have been able to invest in the work of Amor Ministries. Not only has it been a practical and eternal investment in the families who have received new homes, it has produced life-changing dividends for the people of our church.

Recently, we took our pastoral staff on one of these trips for a team missions project. If you ever meet our pastoral team, you'll understand why Paul's leadership challenge is akin to herding cats. As best as possible, we tried to stay out of his way by letting him do what he knows best.

Before crossing the border that morning, we ate breakfast at a fast food restaurant, where Paul briefed us on our assignment and on some of the things we should know and expect to see. He reminded us, for instance, that we were going there to serve—a good reminder for a group of leaders. For those of us who hadn't been to Mexico in awhile, Paul prepared us for the poverty we would see. He also told us about the housing project. The homes made by Amor would cost about $5,000 on the open market, which, for the American housing market, sounds like pocket change. But for the Mexican people, who bring home about $50 a week, these homes serve as precious dwellings for them and their children.

Once we crossed the border, I was able to put a name and a face on how two-thirds of the world lives. After driving up a steep, rocky hill surrounded by various degrees of dilapidated homes in the eastern portion of Tijuana, I got out of the car and met a dark, leather-skinned man named Magdellano. He and his family were to be the recipients of the home we were going to build together. It wasn't *us* building a home for *him*; we had the privilege of working alongside the home *he was building* through the help of Amor. The difference in attitude and perspective is crucial.

Magdellano is not much different from you and me. He wants to provide food, shelter, and a future for his wife, Marianna, and their six children. Building this home was a dream come true for them. We worked side-by-side that day, mixing cement and plastering stucco on the four outside walls of his home. As we worked together in the dusty heat, it made me take a look at my own life, which is the inevitable by-product of missions trips like this. Here was Magdellano, a hard-working guy who had little in the way of material things—in fact, nothing by the standards of Orange County—and yet joy and contentment filled his heart and attitude. He was happy to be getting a small, two-room home with strong walls and a solid roof! By contrast, I thought about how much we have back home, but seldom, if ever, feel content. Something is amiss here.

## The Significance of Simplicity

How is it that you and I live in the richest country in the world but experience a spiritual poverty that is in direct proportion to our material wealth? What is it about our homes, our luxury cars, our in-home entertainment systems, our paid vacations, and the abundance of pleasures we've been blessed with that leave our hearts thirsty, aching for something more? Could it be that the very words of Jesus, mentioned at the beginning of this little book, are whispering to our hearts?

*For where your treasure lies, there you will find your heart.*

Like the many people who went through their garages and closets to sell once-treasured items at the

Treasure Sale, maybe God is calling us to go through the clutter in our hearts and to simplify our lives. Maybe the answer lies in asking ourselves what we attach ourselves to in this life and what treasures are keeping us from experiencing our true freedom in Christ. Maybe the answer for living a life of significance is found in keeping it simple.

*Simplicity* is the fourth sign of significance. It is the practice of finding value in the "little things." In a world that values "bigger and better" as signs of success, God finds greatness in the faithful simplicity of small things born out of a child-like faith in God. In the practice of simplicity, God is the One who gives us the grace to live with less so we might live a fuller life in Him. We live with less so others can live with more. Simplicity frees us to live the unencumbered life of the Spirit, which is attentive to the needs of those around us.

But talking about living a life of simplicity and the significance it brings is next to impossible if we are not willing to look into our hearts and see what pleasures we treasure. We are all creatures of habit and as such, we have our creature comforts. The question we must ask ourselves is simple if we want to get a bearing on living a life of simplicity: Do you and I spend more time pursuing pleasure than storing treasure in heaven? Ouch! That's a tough question, but an essential

THE FOURTH
SIGN OF
SIGNIFICANCE:

*simplicity*

one for living a life of significance. Let's look at many of our simple pleasures in practical terms.

- How many Starbucks lattes or mocha frappuccinos did you buy last month in comparison with money given to help those in need?
- How many movies, DVDs, or videos did you see or rent this year? (We won't get into Blockbuster late fees!)
- What about chocolate addictions or special dinners eating out?
- Does your checkbook or credit card statement reflect Kingdom priorities?
- If you've given your life to Christ, have you given Him your money and possessions as well?

Our list could go on and on, but our purpose is not to lay a heavy guilt trip on you. Our goal is to help you consider the benefits to a life of simplicity, which will lead you to a deeper, albeit lighter, relationship with God.

In Paul's second letter to Timothy, he warns Timothy to be on the lookout for people who claim to be spiritual but who, in fact, are "lovers of pleasure rather than lovers of God—having a form of godliness, but denying its power" (2 Tim. 3:4–5). Could it be that some of us never experience the power of God in our lives because we are lovers of pleasure? We go to church on Sundays. We tip God with the equivalent of ten-cent tithes. We sing inspirational praise songs—all a definite form of godliness as the apostle Paul wrote about—but we never see any real changes in our hearts and lives. Then we wonder why the Christian life isn't all that it's cracked up to be.

We say we treasure God, but are our real pleasures found in our home equity, the boat in the harbor that never gets sailed, drug addiction, or the dead-end romantic relationship we're afraid to let go of?

Simplicity helps us to be grateful people, thankful for the blessings God has showered on us. The beauty of simplicity is found in letting go of all things. As we said in *The Kingdom Assignment*, there's nothing inherently wrong with money or possessions. They are gifts from God for our enjoyment, but we are first to be good stewards of all God gives us, and that means first living with Kingdom priorities.

God calls us to be lovers of Him.

Not lovers of money or treasure or pleasure.

Keeping it simple helps us to do just that.

## A Dog-Gone Determination

Living a life of simplicity isn't just limited to money or possessions. Keeping it simple also means looking at our lifestyle, how busy we are, what consumes our time and energy, and, most important, what keeps us from hearing the voice of the Lord in our lives. For many of us whose lives are marked by busyness and the tyranny of the urgent, a commitment to simplicity requires a specific determination to identify where and when life is getting out of control in order to take steps to eliminate its chaos. Living a life of significance sometimes means making tough choices, rethinking previous decisions, and making new choices in order to simplify our lives.

Tom and Kelly are the parents of two girls and two boys, which means life in their home is a wee bit busy. For years, Megan, their oldest daughter, had been begging her mom and dad for a dog. Unfortunately for her, Megan heard the same answer again and again, "When you're old enough, you can get a dog." Megan felt confused, not knowing when "old enough" would come.

Both Tom and Kelly had grown up in "dog families." They had both had pets as youngsters and knew the large responsibility of owning one. So, before getting a dog for Megan, Tom and Kelly were very clear that this was going to be *her* dog. Megan would be responsible for feeding, training, walking, and playing with the dog, and for picking up what it left in the backyard. Tom and Kelly promised to help and support Megan, but the dog was to be her primary responsibility. They had seen too many families bring home new puppies for kids who'd promised to care for them, but who were eventually let off the hook and it soon became the parents' primary responsibility. Megan's parents vowed not to become codependent dog owners!

"Old enough" came one day after growing weary of hearing Megan's endless whimpers. After searching in the newspaper, Tom and Kelly found a one-year-old yellow lab named Max. They bought the dog for a $150 from a professional couple who didn't have any time for a pet, so that it was left alone most of the day. Thus when Max, the untrained, large, lovable lab was brought to a new home with four children dying to play with a dog, the overgrown pup jumped right in.

When Max met Joseph, Tom and Kelly's five-year-old son, he established an immediate bond by running at him like a racehorse, leaping into the air, and tackling Joseph like an NFL linebacker. Scared and in tears, Joseph welcomed Max into the family by screaming, "I hate that dog!"

It was June, school was almost out, and Megan quickly got to work training Max, teaching him not to tackle unsuspecting siblings, how to sit on command, when to come, and how to retrieve a ball. Within a month, Max changed a lot of his undisciplined ways and settled into the routine of his new home.

For the first three months, Megan spent a lot of time and energy working with Max, but like most puppies, he was still a puppy. Tom and Kelly began to wonder if they bit off more than they could chew because soon the dog was chewing them out of house and home. They laughed when they heard people say, "Having a puppy is just like having a baby." Tom remarked, "I have four children—and no, having a dog is *not* like having a baby. My children have never knocked over our trashcans. My children never ate the patio furniture seat cushions or clawed down the window screens. And my children never chewed through our air-conditioning conduit! Having a dog is *not* like having a child!"

Max was a good, lovable dog, but Tom and Kelly were not ready to make the leap to "Dogs are people too" (which, we know, might be offensive to dog-lovers reading this book). Megan began to feel divided over her Max responsibilities. She loved her dog, but she realized feeding, training, walking, and cleaning up after Max required more time and energy than she originally estimated. She knew she'd be busy in the fall with homework, her volleyball team, and school activities. Also, walking Max before school meant waking up fifteen minutes earlier in the morning than usual. Megan talked over her dilemma with her parents, and they mutually agreed to wait a couple months before making any final decisions. Jessie, Megan's little sister, joined in and volunteered to share some of Megan's responsibilities. A new game plan was devised to accommodate everyone's schedule.

By the time Kingdom Assignment 2 rolled around, almost everyone in the Smith home felt as if they were in the doghouse. Mom and daughter were frustrated and fighting over who fed and walked Max last, the poop wasn't getting picked up, and Tom was on the verge of signing up for an anger-management class every time Max destroyed a new portion of the house. Kelly was upset trying to manage a husband-turned-Doberman Pincher and two girls fighting like a pair of nasty poodles. Joseph, the only one who'd seen this all coming six months earlier with Max's first flying tackle, felt no love lost at the thought of not having to look over his shoulder every time he went into the backyard to play.

Before making any decision, Tom and Kelly made it clear to Megan that they were willing to keep Max and support her in taking care of the dog, but if Max was to stay, he would still be Megan's responsibility. This was one of those "life lessons," and the choice would ultimately be up to Megan.

After much thought and prayer, Megan decided to find Max a new home. Fortunately, Megan had a friend at school whose cousin was looking for a dog. Her friend's cousin had a large home in San Diego with a big backyard, and her dad was a runner looking for a new running partner. While sad to be losing Max, Megan was grateful that Max was going to expend his boundless energy with lots of long runs.

Max was sold for $150, the same price he was bought for—and the money was given to Kingdom Assignment 2. As Tom and Kelly said, "We know that sounds awful—"selling our dog to give money for the poor"—but we knew we had to simplify our lives, and we are glad the money is going to benefit other people. The decision to sell Max was Megan's, but it brought peace to our whole home."

For every parent who has wrestled with guilt over child-raising decisions of work and responsibility like Tom and Kelly, sometimes parents need to step back and ask themselves: "Right now, what is complicating our family life? Where do we need to change course, cut back or reevaluate some previous decisions? Where do we need to simplify? What busyness or chaos or complicating life-circumstances are keeping our family from a life of significance?" Those are dog-gone tough questions to act upon, but they just might lead to peace at home and peace in your hearts.

CHAPTER 6

# *True Greatness*

Sometimes a life of significance begins with a dream. Early in my ministry, I was on the staff of Calvary Community Church in Westlake Village, where I served for five years as a Youth and Associate Pastor. It was in those years that God put a dream in our hearts to start what became Coast Hills Community Church in Orange County, about a hundred miles to the south. A couple in our church, Frank and Susan, heard about our plans to launch this new church and invited us out for dinner. Although Leesa and I didn't know Frank and Susan very well, they were a friendly couple and we were happy to accept.

After the four of us sat down in the restaurant, Frank and Susan asked us to outline our vision for the church and how we saw ourselves making a difference in people's lives through this new ministry. I've always liked open-ended questions like that and I kept talking until our Caesar salads arrived.

As I awkwardly chomped on an unusually large piece of Romaine lettuce, Frank passed a check across the table. I looked up to see a huge smile on his face.

"What's this all about?" I asked.

"You'll see," he said.

I glanced at the numbers scribbled on the check in Frank's hand.

*Eighteen thousand dollars!*

I nearly choked on my salad. "Frank, this is the largest check I've ever seen in my life."

"Good," he said. "I wish it could be bigger."

"But it's so generous. How will we ever be able to thank you?"

"You can't."

"What do you mean?"

"You see, this money isn't ours. It belongs to the Lord, and we sensed that He wants us to share it with you. We believe in what you're doing and want to have a part in it. Use this check as you see fit for getting the church off the ground."

## The Significance of Servanthood

In their minds, Frank and Susan were serving us through their financial giving so that we might serve others. They were first investing in God's Kingdom, and second, as friends, they were investing in our dream of starting a church where the good news of Jesus Christ could be preached to those who'd never heard the gospel before. If Frank and Susan hadn't stepped out in faith and given as the Lord was leading them to, only God knows what obstacles Leesa and I were able to avoid in starting the church. And believe me, we had enough obstacles to begin with!

Through their giving, Frank and Susan demonstrated to us the spirit of *servanthood*, which is the fifth sign of significance. Servanthood is the practice of putting others before yourself. It means letting go of what you treasure in order to meet a need for someone else.

THE FIFTH
SIGN OF
SIGNIFICANCE:

*servanthood*

Servanthood involves different things at different times. Sometimes it involves letting go of treasured *things* in order to be used for others. Sometimes it's letting go of treasured *time* to be invested toward others. Sometimes it may be letting go of a treasured *position* (for example, of privilege or honor) to serve beneath another. But it always involves giving of yourself to benefit or assist someone else.

Jesus is the best example of what it means to be a valued servant in the Kingdom of God. The apostle Paul exhorted the early church to follow Christ's humble actions and attitudes of servanthood. In his letter to the Philippians (2:3–7), Paul writes:

> Do nothing out of selfish ambition or vain conceit, but in humility consider others better than yourselves. Each of you should look not only to your own interests, but also to the interests of others.

Your attitude should be the same as that of Christ Jesus:

*Who, being in very nature God,*
*did not consider equality with God*
*something to be grasped,*
*but made himself nothing,*
*taking the very nature of a servant,*
*being made in human likeness.*

Paul implies that if anyone had a right to be served, it was Jesus. The Bible tells us that Jesus is the supreme "King of kings," yet Jesus, God's own Son, made himself a servant. Even while Christ existed as fully divine in nature and character, he chose to come and live among us as a servant. A plate scrubber and towel bearer. Therein lies greatness, from God's Kingdom perspective.

Paul goes on to write that as a result of Jesus' obedient servanthood, an obedience that took him to the cross, God the Father

*exalted [Jesus] to the highest place*
*and gave him the name that is above every name,*
*that at the name of Jesus every knee should bow ...*
*and every tongue confess that Jesus Christ is Lord,*
*to the glory of God the Father. (Phil. 2:9–11)*

Jesus demonstrated the value and importance of servanthood before His own disciples. In John 13, when He celebrated the Passover with His disciples, He modeled the significant life of servanthood by setting aside the right position of honor due Him and took up a water basin and towel to wash their feet. When He was finished, Jesus took the opportunity to tell them—and us—exactly what He was doing and why:

> "Do you understand what I have done for you?" he asked them. "You call me 'Teacher' and 'Lord,' and rightly so, for that is what I am. Now that I, your Lord and Teacher, have washed your feet, you also should wash one another's feet. I have set you an example that you should do as I have done for you. I tell you the truth, no servant is greater than his master, nor is a messenger greater than the one who sent him. Now that you know these things, you will be blessed if you do them." (John 13: 12–17)

## The Church in Action

It may be hard for many of us to imagine becoming busboys for the Kingdom of God, but I believe we may never be more *like* Jesus, especially in the eyes of others, than when we give of ourselves to serve others. William Barclay, a renowned Bible teacher and commentator, said this about the significance of servanthood:

> The world may assess a man's greatness by the number of people whom he controls and who are at his beck and call; or by his intellectual standing and his academic eminence; or by the number of committees of which he is a member; or by the size of one's bank balance and assets and the material possessions which he has amassed; but in the assessment of Jesus Christ these

are irrelevant. His assessment is quite simply this . . . How many people has he served? Therein lies greatness!

I remember being interviewed by one of the producers of *Dateline NBC* during the excitement generated in our church during our first Kingdom Assignment. In a rather candid moment, she asked me why we were doing this project. I hesitated before responding, but then answered with something I believe now with all my heart: "I think the world is sick and tired of *hearing* from the church."

By the look on her face, it wasn't what she expected to hear from a pastor. So I explained myself further. "What the world needs, I suspect, is to *see* the church be who we say we are. And that, inescapably, involves serving Christ by practically serving others, especially 'the least of these' among us." That is our challenge and our most compelling reason and defense of our faith, before a watching and often skeptical world.

To become the servants God is calling us to be, you and I must wrestle with the truth that there is always a cost in coming to Jesus and following him in a significant way. In Luke 9, Jesus addressed a small group of men who were caught up in the excitement of His growing ministry. Walking alongside Jesus, the first man bolted out, "I will follow you wherever you go." Almost immediately, Jesus recognized the man's limitations on the meaning of "wherever." He reminded the man that following Him might cost him his *comfort*.

*If we're going to follow Jesus, He may ask us to give up some comforts.*

The next man's plea was, "Let me go bury my father first." On the surface, it doesn't seem like such an unusual or outlandish request. But Jesus apparently sensed this was more an issue of *convenience* than loyalty to family. Had his father just passed away, or was the potential follower talking about something in the vague future? Jesus wanted to make clear that the cost to follow Jesus was one of time and allegiance.

*If we're going to follow Jesus, He may ask us to give up some convenience.*

A third man requested the desire to go back and say goodbye to his loved ones. Again, that's not what you would call a terrible thing, but Jesus sensed a level of *commitment* that suggested this man would always be looking back, wondering what unfinished business or opportunity he might have left behind.

*If we are going to follow Jesus, He may ask us to give up a certain commitment.*

Comfort. Convenience. Commitment.

These are the real issues and the real obstacles to living a life of significance. The common denominator among these three incidents is our daily need to consider the cost in following Jesus. You see, maybe no one has told you this, but there is a definite cost to following Jesus. There always has been. There always will be. The cost will come in different ways, but there will always be a specific, significant cost because it is the only way that leads to the significant relationship that Jesus modeled and desires to have with each of us.

## The Joy of Servanthood

By this time, you may be having second thoughts or doubts whether it's really possible to live a life of significance as Jesus promised. If so, you are not alone. Getting out of your comfort zone and taking new, bold steps of faith is scary (as we said in the first statements of this book, *dangerous*), but it's also exciting when you see the life change it produces in your heart and in the lives of those you serve. If you have a sneaky little fear that a life of servanthood leads to a dull and dreary existence of being somebody else's doormat to wipe their feet, then let us politely demolish that misconception by talking about the wonderful joy servanthood produces. Why? Because we have so many stories of joy to prove it.

Kingdom Assignment 2 provided every one of the thousand participants great opportunities for spiritual growth through serving others. When Christ-followers store up treasure in heaven by serving others with their talents, money, and time, the Holy Spirit provides a deep satisfaction known only by those who have had the privilege of being a servant. This satisfaction is the spiritual fruit of joy, and it is an essential characteristic of those who serve in the name of Christ. Again and again, we saw countless individuals—whole families even—surprised at how much their joy increased in direct proportion to their giving and serving. When we asked

Kingdom Assignment 2 participants what they learned in the process of selling a treasured possession and serving others in the name of Christ, here are some of the joy-filled discoveries they made along the way:

> *The more one tries to achieve wealth and accumulate "things," the more stressful and "unfun" life becomes. Things and money don't make a person; God and family do.*
>
> —Charlie & Chris

> *In Kingdom Assignment 2, I realized that there is a contest going on for my attention and loyalties.*
>
> —Lorenz

> *Too often, we become attached to things rather than Christ. We use "stuff" to fill up the God-shaped hole in our hearts. If we don't take care of "the least of these," then we don't understand God's plan for us.*
>
> —Vern & Karen

> *Kingdom Assignment 2 reminded me that material things are really insignificant in relationship to the big picture of God's Kingdom.*
>
> —Lynette

> *There is always someone in greater need, and by giving up something that may have been a value to you, it will be of even greater value and help to someone else and therefore serve an even greater purpose.*
>
> —Lori

*If we give what's left over, the church feeds neither us spiritually nor anyone else. If we give "dues," our church is no more than a club to us. If we give the same as we always have, we can only expect declining returns.*

—Sharon

Living lives of servanthood not only produces a deep, lasting joy and leads us to a life of significance, it can also produce some significant, unexpected surprises. Surprises that, in earthly terms, don't always seem to add up.

# CHAPTER 7

# *Kingdom Math*

As a young man growing up in junior high and high school, there was really only one subject I didn't get or care for … *math!* Whether sitting in class watching my teacher scribble on the chalkboard or doing my homework at the kitchen table, to be honest, I just didn't get it! In fact, in the ninth grade, I remember my algebra teacher signing my yearbook, "To the 'I-Don't-Get-It' Kid!"

At the time, not only did I not understand the intricacies of sophisticated mathematics, like algebra and trigonometry. I also never saw any particular reason why I was personally ever going to need to "get it," except for getting correct change from the Coke machine.

But over the last several years, I've begun to see a wonderful scenario where numbers and equations *are* fun and important. It's what I call *Kingdom Math*, and it's when God's Kingdom is being extended and expanded at a rate that's almost impossible to measure. When people choose to do something significant in the name of Christ and begin to live lives of significance, it is amazing to see the multiplying examples of life change that can happen. *When people get it by putting their faith into action, God's work is multiplied beyond our wildest dreams.*

One of the great passages on Kingdom Math is found in the Gospel of Mark. Jesus is teaching His disciples a parable, a story from everyday life with a profound spiritual lesson to convey. He says:

> "Listen! A farmer went out to sow his seed. As he was scattering the seed, some fell along the path, and the birds came and ate it up. Some fell on rocky places, where it did not have much soil. It sprang up quickly, because the soil was shallow. But when the sun came up, the plants were scorched, and they withered because they had no root. Other seed fell among thorns, which grew up and choked the plants, so that they did not bear grain. Still other seed fell on good soil. It came up, grew and produced a crop, multiplying thirty, sixty, or even a hundred times." (Mark 4:3–8)

*30x . . . 60x . . . 100x.*

100x . . . now that's a kind of mathematical equation I get excited about!

In Southern California, Leesa and I witness the 100x phenomenon every spring. Around March and early April, the hills of Southern California become covered with the beautiful, bright yellow flowers of mustard plants. The seed of a mustard plant is very small, about the size of a pinhead, but what it can produce is astounding. As we drive the freeways or side roads, brilliant yellow flowers fill the hills with magnificent radiance. All it took was just some seed scattered to the wind multiplied a million times over.

What's interesting about this Kingdom Math is that it's not so much dependent on what we do as much as on what God wants to do and is capable of doing through us. Don't you think that is what Jesus was getting at when he talked about our lives producing 30x, 60x, and 100x in other people's lives? How amazing it would be if our lives produced as much brilliance and beauty as those yellow covered hills!

On the surface, the Parable of the Sower and the Seed is a simple story about a farmer who goes out to sow seed in his fields. But the story isn't about seed ... it's a story about soil. Jesus compares each of the four soils to the four conditions of people's hearts and their readiness to receive the Word of God. He describes the different kinds of soil the seed falls onto and what each of these soils yield at the harvest. Of the first group of people, He says:

> Some people are like seed along the path, where the word is sown. As soon as they hear it, Satan comes and takes away the word that was sown in them. (Mark 4:15)

These people, Jesus said, are *hard-hearted*. There is no receptivity in them to what God's Word says, and because of their hearts, their lives produce nothing. The seed is useless and lost.

Of the second group of people, Jesus says:

> Others, like seed sown on rocky places, hear the word
> and at once receive it with joy. But since they have no
> root, they last only a short time. When trouble or per-
> secution comes because of the word, they quickly fall
> away. (Mark 4:16–17).

These people, Jesus said, are *shallow-hearted*. While they
may have a willingness to receive the Word and every
intention of it producing a harvest through them, they
have no roots, and often, just as quickly, they fall away.
Their potential is short-lived and fades when disap-
pointment, trial, or trouble comes their way.

In describing the third group of people, Jesus says:

> Still others, like seed sown among thorns, hear the
> word; but the worries of this life, the deceitfulness of
> wealth and the desires for other things come in and
> choke the word, making it unfruitful. (Mark 4: 18–19)

These people, Jesus said, are *crowded-hearted*. They *want*
to see the Word produce a harvest in them, but they are dis-

THE SIXTH
SIGN OF
SIGNIFICANCE:

*surprise*

tracted by "the worries of this life,
the deceitfulness of wealth and the
desire for other things" that call
and clamor for their attention.
These people have many treasures
and pleasures and, like RYR, they
have yet to surrender their *one
thing* to Jesus.

Of the final group of people, Jesus says:

> Others, like seed sown on good soil, hear the word, accept it, and produce a crop—thirty, sixty or even a hundred times what was sown. (Mark 4:20)

These people, Jesus said, are *tender-hearted*. The Word of God finds a warm reception in their hearts and lives, and the choices and actions of their lives reflect that condition. These are people who have identified their *one thing*, letting it go in service of God's Kingdom, and they are well on their way to a life of significance.

And here's the clincher.

The tender-hearted are *surprised* by the great harvest God produces in their lives.

## The Significance of Surprise

*Surprise* is the sixth sign in the life of those who chose a life of significance. It is the sign of God's hand and power at work in multiplying exceedingly more than they could have ever hoped or imagined. It's what the apostle Paul had in mind when he penned these words to the church in Ephesus:

> Now to him who is able to do immeasurably more than all we ask or imagine, according to his power that is at work within us, to him be glory in the church and in Christ Jesus throughout all generations, for ever and ever! Amen. (Eph. 3:20–21)

When we initiated Kingdom Assignment 2, we had eyes to see what it could become, having experienced what we did the first time around in Kingdom Assignment 1, but God had a way of multiplying and bringing about more surprises than we could have ever hoped or dreamed. *That's Kingdom Math!*

How He does it, that I'll never get.

## The Great Giveaway

It was during the 2001 Thanksgiving weekend when we held the collection for Kingdom Assignment 2. In one way or another the people of Coast Hills demonstrated the signs of significance we mentioned so far. Sacrifice. Surrender. Submission. Simplicity. Servanthood. We were encouraged as the envelopes were opened the Monday after Thanksgiving. Included in the envelopes people had written to us stories of the treasured possessions they sold for the poor. Their simple efforts brought about a sense of surprise to us as we sat and read story after story of their faithfulness. Over the next few weeks more monies trickled in, and when it was all said and done, $110,000 was in the bank and ready for distribution.

Our goal was to help the poor in our area and to give it to reputable local organizations that would handle it in a way pleasing to God. We hosted a luncheon for city council members and mayors in our surrounding area, asking them for their ideas and opinions concerning the best organizations to give money to. We had a few ideas of our own, but it was a great way to partner with our neighbors and get their input.

When the day came to distribute the money, it couldn't have been better timing. It was right before Christmas, when the local charities needed the money the most. Many organizations matched our giving, multiplying it even more.

Habitat for Humanity, Saddleback Community Outreach, Agape House, Family Resource Center of Aliso Viejo, Orange County Boys and Girls Programs, Young Life Camping Fund, Winter Care for the Homeless, Community Resource Network—all received amounts ranging from $5,000 to $10,000. These are all organizations that help those in need of food, shelter, family counseling, and resources to compete in the job market.

These were not just organizations we helped out monetarily, but they were also places our congregation could serve firsthand. Putting on hard hats, forty-five men, women, and children from Coast Hills had the opportunity to build homes right along side their new owners one Saturday in December for Habitat for Humanity. The list went on to include $10 food vouchers handed out randomly in front of grocery stores to stimulate the local economy and extend a gift to our community. Our local newspaper, the *Orange County Register*, provided an opportunity through their "Season of Caring" program by matching our gift and providing financial assistance to up to fifty local reputable organizations. To keep our staff members on their servanthood toes, ten of our pastors received $500 each to multiply and give out to families in need within their area of ministry. It was a true joy to experience and watch God's people get excited about.

Then something surprising happened. After distributing over $100,000 into the community, we still had $10,000 more. As we sat around the conference table and bounced around ideas, a staff member brilliantly piped up: "What do you think if we gave another $100 dollars to another hundred people and see what God does again."

In December 2001, Eric Nachtrieb, our Pastor of Missions, was given the fun job of handing out the $10,000. After Kingdom Assignment 1, people told us they were sad they missed out the first time. When he asked for volunteers this day, hands shot up all through the congregation, ready and willing to take on the assignment. Some even got out of their seat and ran toward him to grab the $100 bills before they were all gone. There was no lack of enthusiasm, and again, we felt the buzz and curiosity of what God was going to do this time around.

One hundred individuals each took $100 of God's money, multiplied it, and scattered it to those in need.

The 100x phenomenon worked in a powerful way:

- $2,500 raised to establish a fund for disabled children in memory of a disabled sister who passed away five years ago
- $10,275 raised for thirty scholarships to send disadvantaged kids to camp

- $2,225 raised for Laura's House, a home for abused women and children
- $9,000 raised for Project Home, which helps homeless children in Orange County
- $1,000 raised for Kathy's House, a home for women in transition
- $525 raised for a son of a coworker who was dying and in need of assistance
- $9,000 raised by one couple who enlisted a hundred of their friends to give to a fund for widows and the fatherless
- $100,000 raised by fifty people who purchased and participated in repairing a home for a single mother of four whose husband had died
- $1,000 raised for a reading project for needy kids
- $1,050 raised for the Coast Hills Food Pantry, which feeds 450 families biweekly
- $1,350 raised by ten people to assist a single mom with preschool tuition so she could work
- $1,000 raised to help Trinity Law School students
- $160 raised by a mom who distributed $20 bills with her children to the homeless on Hollywood Boulevard
- $100 given to a house painter who needed work
- $500 raised for twenty-five "Birthday Goody Bags" for the elderly at a local Senior Center

*Want to see Kingdom Math at work?* This $10,000 was scattered, sown, and multiplied into a total of $209,384!

All by moms and dads, singles and teenagers, children and seniors. People with rocky marriages, financial stress, struggles at work, serious health issues, overdue bills, crazy teenagers, and doubts about God. People who would give anything to lose that last ten pounds, yet who wanted more out of life than just stuff. Normal, everyday people who chose significance over success and were surprised as anyone at the incredible harvest. Where did they get the heart and the perspective and the grace to accomplish such great things for God's Kingdom?

In 2 Corinthians 9:8–11, Paul writes about the source of all Kingdom Assignments:

> And God is able to make all grace abound to you, so that in all things at all times, having all that you need, you will abound in every good work.... Now he who supplies seed to the sower and bread for food will also supply and increase your store of seed and will enlarge the harvest of your righteousness. You will be made rich in every way so that you can be generous on every occasion, and through us your generosity will result in thanksgiving to God.

Notice the blessings promised in these verses: "all grace ... all things ... all times ... all you need." Plenty of supply ... increased as necessary ... enlarged and harvested all to one end ... more generosity and more ministry that brings more glory and more praise and more thanksgiving to God. Wow!

When God started answering prayer, we were flooded with stories. Stories of tender-hearted people on whom

God has scattered His seed far and wide. 100x stories of life change, creativity, transformation . . . and, well, an amazing harvest all to the glory of God.

## A Ton of Fun Brings in Three Tons of Food

John and Lisa were new Christians when they scooped up one of the new assignments $100 bills. Young in their faith and excited to see this money multiplied for the needy, they went home and talked about how this money could assist the poor, but nothing seemed to come to mind. So they decided to pray.

On the same evening, Lisa came across an article in a local newspaper, which explained that because of the difficult economic times following September 11, the local Salvation Army didn't have enough food to assist the needy at Christmas. That was all the spark that John and Lisa needed to ignite a flame of action. They decided to use the $100 to print fliers to distribute to the four hundred homes in their gated community. On the fliers, John and Lisa explained that they were having a "One Hour Food Drive" at their home in one week. They went door to door with their kids and hand-delivered the fliers, wondering what would happen the following week. What transpired was truly amazing. John and Lisa and their kids went all out, got right into the Christmas spirit, decorated the tree, and even hired Dickens Carolers dressed in their finest to sing as neighbors arrived lugging bags of groceries.

At the appointed time, not one by one but by hoards, the whole neighborhood began to show up. One family went to Costco and filled their Suburban full of food. Another guy came by, saw the Food Drive sign out in front, stopped, and wrote a check for $200. Another lady stopped by pulling a little red wagon filled with food. Even the local supermarkets got into the act, donating $20 and $25 gift certificates. In sixty minutes of joyful and generous pandemonium, this family collected over 6,000 pounds of food. *That's three tons of food!*

When the Salvation Army truck came to haul the food away, were they ever elated and surprised! They were able to fill their storehouses and fill many tummies during the holiday season.

## Sweatshirts with a Message

One woman decided she wanted to help the homeless for her Kingdom Assignment. After multiplying her $100, she and a friend purchased black, hooded sweatshirts with John 3:16 printed on it. But not to confuse it by your average Joe at an NFL Football game, she actually printed out the whole verse on the front of the sweatshirt:

> *FOR GOD SO LOVED THE WORLD THAT HE GAVE HIS ONE AND ONLY SON, THAT WHOEVER BELIEVES IN HIM SHALL NOT PERISH BUT HAVE ETERNAL LIFE.*

Not only did these homeless men see the Scripture verse every day, but they also became walking billboards, preaching faith in Christ for all to see. The sweatshirt provided physical warmth to those who wore it and spiritual warmth to all who read it. Who knows how God will multiply its effects for eternity?

## A College Bound Two-Year-Old

Christine took a wonderfully creative Kingdom Math approach by writing letters to many friends and relatives, asking them to pass on an idea she had for helping a woman in need with a two-year-old daughter. This is a portion from the thank-you letter Christine sent out to all who participated:

> *Dear Family and Friends,*
> *I just want to thank you all from the bottom of my heart for participating in my "Kingdom Assignment" to raise money for a College Savings plan for my friend Erin's two-year-old daughter, Darian. As you all know, Erin has advanced cancer. She is still fighting the cancer "tooth and nail" today, but with an amazing positive spirit and attitude. She is so grateful for all the prayers and support she has received from all of you and so am I. Together, we were able to raise $8,500 dollars for her daughter!*

That $8,500 now has a fifteen-year head start to grow before Darian starts college. It all started with a fertile heart and a hundred bucks! Can't you see the 30x, 60x, 100x in these people's lives?

## Kingdom Math through the Pages

After our first book, *The Kingdom Assignment: What Will You Do with the Talents God Has Given You?*

churches, organizations, and people from all over the world began taking on the Kingdom Assignment challenge. Daily we would receive messages of surprise of God's faithfulness in others lives, not just in our own church.

One day, a call came into the Coast Hills office from a guy named Brent from San Antonio, Texas. He left a message and said it was of utmost importance that one of us calls him back. When I called and said, "Hi, Brent, this is Leesa Bellesi returning your call," his first response was, "I read your stupid book."

I sensed he was joking, but I wasn't sure, so I paused waiting for him to go on. Brent explained that he was a director of a Young Life group in San Antonio. Young Life is an international youth ministry organization dedicated to sharing the gospel with unchurched students. Brent had read the book and felt God was leading him to take $1,000 out of his personal savings and hand out $25 dollars to forty of his students. Even though he and his wife were struggling financially, Brent obeyed what God was calling him to do.

The surprise? The morning *after* Brent and his wife handed out the $1,000 from their personal savings, he arrived in his office to find an unexpected check made out to them for $1,000. We can't outgive God, can we?

We received many letters, a few of which we'd like to share with you so you can see how simple it is to start a Kingdom Assignment of your own:

*I sat down to read your book. The next thing I know, it's midnight and my wife was wondering what I was doing up so late, but still I kept reading. I couldn't put your book down until I finished it. I am now working on two Kingdom Assignment projects. One for my students, at the Catholic church were I teach CCD and one for people in NYC, with people who may or may not have been impacted by the World Trade Center tragedy on September 11. I am creating a journal of my actions. Thank you for your book. Though you are in California and I am in New York, I feel as if you are right next door. You have made a difference in my life. Now as God's servant, I hope to make a difference in others.*

Robert in the Bronx, New York

*An individual in our community read a newspaper article about the Kingdom Assignment and came and offered me $5,000 dollars for the same purpose in our church.*

*I read the book and we were off and running.*

*It has been almost a month since we initiated our kingdom assignment. It has caused no small stir in this little small town of Magnolia. Most people have taken it very seriously and are each looking into it in so many different ways. Some are looking into helping student missionaries; one person is interested in starting a crisis pregnancy center (with lots of response there); one lady started a fund for the National Day of Prayer and within four days she was able to raise over a thousand dollars. Many are still praying and seeking God's guidance. But most everyone quickly picked up on the opportunity to invest the money and have found people to join them in this most extraordinary assignment.*

Pastor Wood in Magnolia, Arkansas

*My wife, Margaret, and I are the children and youth ministers at our church and we have a group of kids who need a ride. We turned our $1,000 into $15,000 and were able to purchase a twenty-seven-passenger bus for our church. The bus ministry is in the beginning stages, but the potential is enormous. God truly blessed our sacrifice. Not only did the money come in, but also our ministry was enhanced because of the time we spent one-on-one with families that helped raise the money along side us.*

Jeff and Margaret from Tulsa, Oklahoma

## Kingdom Math Provides Hope

If you had an opportunity to read our first book, you will remember the story of Terry. Terry was a married mother of four who lived in an affluent neighborhood. Terry knew that much was expected of her since God had blessed her with so many things. She multiplied the $100 that was given to her and helped a woman by the name of Lisa. God developed a wonderful and extraordinary friendship between Terry and Lisa, but that's not the end of the story . . . it's not even close to being the end of the story.

Terry and Lisa's friendship propelled what we consider to be a 100x vision initiated by Kay Barker, our Women's Ministry Director. About a year before the

Kingdom Assignment happened, Kay began dreaming and praying about developing a home for women in transition with financial needs like Lisa. When Terry and Lisa told their story on the night of our Kingdom Assignment Celebration in February 2001, Terry shared this dream to build a home called Hope's House. No one knew of the surprises God had in store for creating just such a home.

A month later, a gentleman who heard Kay and Terry's vision that evening anonymously gave $75,000 as a down payment for Hope's House. In the next several months that followed, through the help of the media, our Woman's Ministry, Coast Hills Executive Pastor Rick Dunn, local businesses, volunteers, and Terry's persistence to bring it all together, an amazing $350,000 was raised to buy, remodel, and redecorate a small apartment building.

On the anniversary of our first Kingdom Assignment, November 4, 2001, Hope's House opened its doors. The two little children of Hope's House first resident family ran from bedroom to bedroom screaming and laughing, completely surprised and amazed to be sleeping in their own beds! After all the long months of hard work drywalling, painting, and decorating the apartment units, the brilliant mustard seed laughter of two children singing and dancing on their beds filled Hope's House with an immeasurable harvest of joy.

*Will your one thing, your one treasure or pleasure, ever satisfy like that?*

Whoever sows sparingly will also reap sparingly, and whoever sows generously will also reap generously. (2 Cor. 9:6)

When God's people open their hearts and allow His seed to fall on fertile, tender hearts, the 100x harvest can be an overwhelming and an incredible surprise.

And it all begins by listening to what God encourages us to do according to His Word.

# CHAPTER 8

# A Call To Action

One weekend, I was scheduled to officiate the wedding of a close high school friend of our daughter, Brooke. The wedding was scheduled on a Saturday afternoon the first weekend in November in Walnut Creek, not far from Oakland and San Francisco. Since the Bay Area is only a one-hour plane flight from Orange County, I figured I could be home on Saturday afternoon following the wedding reception.

I normally do not accept out-of-town invitations, but Amy's family are dear friends of ours—and perhaps the prospect of an Italian wedding with all that great food tipped my decision. The only thing that made me hesitate was that Brooke was pregnant and due to deliver her first baby in late November. But then again, thirty days between Amy's wedding and the birth of my first grandchild shouldn't cause any problems. Right?

After the rehearsal dinner on Friday evening, I called home to check in.

The answering machine picked up, which was strange, since it was after 10 P.M.

"Hi, you've reached the Bellesis, and if this is Denny, your daughter is on the way to the hospital. We're gonna have a baby!"

"How can Brooke be in labor?" I wondered. "She isn't due for a whole month?"

I dialed Leesa's cell phone number, and sure enough, she was at the hospital.

"Can you come home?" she pleaded. "I've always dreamed we would be holding hands hearing our first grandchild cry for the first time. This is important."

"Honey, you know I can't. There's no way. Anyway, it's too late. The Oakland Airport is closed and there are no flights coming or going until the morning. Besides, I have this wedding tomorrow. I can't just leave. You know that."

"I know, Denny, but Brooke could deliver the baby tonight, and you won't be here."

I felt horrible. I wanted to be home with my family for such a momentous event, but I was stuck in Walnut Creek. "I'm sorry, honey, but I don't see how I can get there. Even if I rented a car, it would take nine hours to drive home."

Two hours later, my already troubled sleep was disturbed by another phone call from Leesa.

"Denny, it would be really great if you could be here," she said. As you might imagine, it wasn't a fun conversation. I agreed with Leesa, but what could I do?

At 2:30 in the morning, I received a call from Claudine James, the wife of one of our church elders and one of Leesa's best friends. This was not a good sign. "Your family really needs you," she said.

"I know, Claudine, but it's just not possible."

I barely slept until I received still another phone call at 4:30. It was Leesa again, but now she was crying, "We need you, Denny. Is there anyway you can make it?"

I sat on the edge of my bed, sick to my stomach, weighing my options. I didn't think there was a way, but I had to give it a shot. I called the airlines. Southwest had a flight leaving for John Wayne Airport at 6:05 A.M. with a return flight to the Bay Area leaving at 11:20 A.M. If I made the return flight, I could still make the afternoon wedding.

By this time, it was a few minutes after 5 A.M. The Oakland Airport was thirty-five minutes away with no traffic, but since September 11 was still fresh in everyone's minds, getting through security in a few minutes was going to be impossible.

In a fit of craziness, I threw on my clothes from the previous night. I didn't brush my teeth, didn't comb my hair, ran down to the lobby, and hopped in a cab at 5:15 A.M.

"Listen," I said breathlessly. "I need to be on a flight that leaves at 6:05. If you can get me there on time, I'll give you a huge tip." That's all the encouragement the cab driver needed. We took every corner on two wheels, but as we entered the airport, we hit predawn traffic backup. We were stuck. It was ten minutes to six.

"Isn't there anything we can do?" I asked.

"I know other way," said the cab driver in accented English. He jerked the van into a U-turn, jumped a curb, took some back roads, and finally dumped me in front of the Southwest departure zone at 5:55 A.M. I had ten minutes before the plane left.

"Thanks," I said, throwing him a hundred dollars. I sprinted for the security checkpoint. I didn't have any luggage—just my wallet and a faxed confirmation. I passed through the security line quickly and ran to my gate just as the last passengers were boarding. Within three minutes, I was on board, and the plane departed on time. Whew! This was beginning to feel like a Steve Martin movie.

I landed at John Wayne at 7:35 A.M. and made a mad dash for the taxi stand. "Here, all I have is $27. Get me to St. Joseph's Hospital as fast as you can!"

Twenty minutes later, I ran through the hospital lobby, burst into Brooke's room, who looked up from her bed and said with tears welling in her eyes, "My daddy's here!"

At that moment, I knew I had made the right decision. Our family reunion exchanged hugs and kisses around the room. I took one of the nurses aside and said, "Listen, I have a plane to catch at 11:20, so if you could get busy, I would appreciate it."

Leesa wanted to know if anyone in Walnut Creek knew I was here.

"No one knows I'm gone," I replied.

"Don't you think you should call someone?"

"Good idea." I called the father of the bride, Aldo Pel-lichiotti. "Aldo, I don't want to alarm you, but I'm in Orange County."

"You're where?" he said sounding confused—which was understandable, seeing as I had been at the rehearsal dinner the night before.

"Listen, Brooke went into labor, and I need to be here. I promise that I'll be there for the wedding, but I want you to keep this between you and me."

"Sure, sure," he agreed.

"I need someone to pick me up in Oakland," I said, as we made out a plan.

At 10:30, Brooke was in transition, and I was told it would be at least an hour.

*Well, at least I got here*, I thought, as I started to say my good-byes. I was outside Brooke's room when Leesa and I heard our son-in-law, Darren, say, "Okay, Honey, push!"

Two minutes later, a nurse told us, "Stick around. We might be able to do this after all."

At 10:50, while Leesa and I held hands with our ears pressed against the labor room wall, baby Caeden William King was born. All six pounds and ten ounces of him. Five minutes later, we were allowed in to see this beautiful little boy and pray a blessing over him. I kissed everyone good-bye and ran to meet a waiting car.

We arrived at John Wayne at 11:15 A.M. and, like the last Southwest flight, made it onto the plane as they were shutting the door. In Oakland, I was the first one off the plane and broke into a full run once I got outside, not even breaking stride as my ride pulled up. I arrived back at my hotel, showered, dressed, and arrived at the wedding fifteen minutes before the start. Calm ... cool ... and collected.

I stood in front of the congregation and winked at Aldo—exhausted, but warm with memories of the last twelve hours.

And to think, I almost missed it!

Even though it was a crazy and whirlwind experience, I've never doubted for a moment that it wasn't all worth it because being present for the birth of my first grandchild was one of the most significant moments in my family's life and mine.

Looking back on that time now, I remember there was a moment in that hotel room when I sat in silence on the edge of my bed, trying to get a bearing on what I should do. At that moment, I ruled out the many voices that were vying for my attention and listened for the still, small voice of God. It was a voice that deserved my attention.

## The Significance of Silence

The seventh and final sign of significance is *silence*. The still, small voice of God speaks to us throughout the day, but we only receive the instruction, comfort, and direction of the Lord as we take the time to listen. As unlikely as it may sound in the action-oriented society we live in, silence is the best place to begin to find significance with God.

*silence*

As we explained in the last chapter about the four possible conditions of the human heart to receive the Word of God, it is only the *tender-hearted* follower of Christ who listens and who sees God produce a harvest of 30x, 60x, or 100x in his or her life. The *hard-hearted* person, flat out, doesn't listen to God. The *shallow-hearted* person listens to God only when it's safe, easy, or convenient. The *crowded-hearted* person is too busy pursuing pleasure to listen to God. But the *tender-hearted* person listens to God, accepts His Word, and experiences a powerful, significant life marked by a bountiful harvest of love and good deeds.

Silence is an essential, critical sign in the life of every follower of Christ.

- It is in silence that our conversation with God, our prayer life, is nurtured.
- It is in silence that we worship God in humble reverence and awe.
- It is in silence that we read and study and take the Word of God into our hearts.
- It is in silence that we confess our sin and need for God, receiving full and complete forgiveness through the blood of Jesus Christ.

- It is in silence that we still our hearts, detaching ourselves from the talons of this world's system and asking God to grow in us a simple, holy, authentic love for Him and others.
- It is in silence that we bring all of our needs and wants and petitions before His holy throne, asking for the grace to yield to His good and perfect will.
- It is in silence that we surrender our many *one things* over to Him and ask Him to renew our hearts every day.
- *And it is in silence that we listen.*

Every story we have told in this book about God at work in the lives of so many people giving of themselves and blessing others in the name of Christ all comes down to listening. None of Kingdom Assignments 1 or 2 would have happened without God working through people like you and me, who simply listened to Him.

## A Reminder to Listen

The pastoral staff at Coast Hills has a New Year's resolution: Every January, we go away for a weekend for what we call a "Leadership Advance." Staff members and key church volunteers attend the annual event, which provides everyone an opportunity to refocus and recast our vision for the coming year. At our most recent advance, Nick Taylor, one of our pastors at Coast Hills, taught on experiencing the ministry of the Holy Spirit. Nick focused, above all, on listening to God.

As everyone gathered for the morning's general session, Nick began by saying, "Let me encourage you to slow down and listen, to actually take the Scripture, 'Be still, and know that I am God' seriously."

What Nick said next caused me to sit straighter in my chair. "To help us slow down, I'm going to introduce an exercise called *Lectio Divina*, which is Latin for 'diving reading.'"

A murmur swept through his audience. *What was he talking about?*

"Listen, this is not some New Age mumbo jumbo. *Lectio Divina* was a practice initiated by the ancient fathers of the early church in an effort to help people connect and go deeper in their personal experience with God and His Word." Nick could tell that he was encountering some resistance. To be honest, I wasn't too sure about this type of stuff since I'm a more pragmatic than mystical kind of person. I hoped this wasn't going to be one of those "touchy-feely" moments, which would have driven me nuts—or sent me out of the room looking for coffee. But it wasn't because of what happened next.

"Let's try *Lectio Divina* out on a passage of Scripture," Nick said. "Turn in your Bible to Matthew 18, starting with verse 16. Everyone there?"

To my surprise, this was Matthew's account of the Rich Young Ruler! Since Leesa and I were right in the middle of writing this book on the very same encounter, I immediately thought that maybe God wanted to say something significant to me about my own relationship with Him. Not that I never heard from God before or sensed His direction in my life. When we began Coast Hills Community Church, for instance, I very definitely sensed God *speaking* to me. It's just that I didn't experience that type of communication very often. God could speak, but I tended to think it was always up to Him to get my attention, not necessarily up to me to give Him *my* attention.

As Nick read the passage aloud the first time, he challenged us to focus on one word or phrase that God placed before us.

So I asked myself, "What word, Lord, do you want me to focus on? What phrase should jump out at me?"

After a few minutes, a still, small thought came to my attention.

The first word was *hard*.

The second word was *rich*.

Then the whole phrase came to mind: "How *hard* it is for a *rich* man to enter the kingdom of heaven."

Just why those words came to me at the time, I can't tell you.

Then Nick read the passage aloud to us a second time. This time, he reminded us to ask the Holy Spirit to reveal *why* that word or phrase was important to us or how it connected with us in some way at this time in our life.

*Why indeed?* I thought. As I sat silently reflecting on this verse for several minutes, another verse of Scripture came to mind. It was from Jesus' Sermon on the Mount.

*"Blessed are the poor in spirit, for theirs is the kingdom of heaven"* (Matt. 5:3).

As I sat there focusing on these two different verses, I was struck for the first time by the contrast between the two. On the one hand, how hard it is for a certain kind of person to experience what God has to offer; on the other hand, how ready and receptive another kind of person is to what God will give them.

*What does this have to do with me, Lord,* I wondered?

What slowly came to mind was the realization that I tended to value my *richness* more than my *poorness*. Not so much materially, although I am certainly not above having and liking nice things, even expensive things. This seemed to have more to do with me personally, on the inside, in my spirit. I began to see the place I often go to: to my abilities, my accomplishments, my comforts, my opportunities, my victories, my strengths, my position, my reputation—all of which are, in effect, my *riches*.

As I sat and thought about it, I realized anyone could have such nice and wonderful treasures and still never connect with God. No, to receive and drink from the pool of God's amazing grace, I needed to connect in some way with my *poorness*—with my sin, my shortcomings, my failures, my fears, my weaknesses, and my barriers. I needed to be in touch with my spiritual poverty so that I could realize and appreciate all the more my need and love for God.

As I reflected on this more, I began to see that I had it all backwards. I want to be rich at the expense of being poor—financially rich, materially rich, intellectually rich, socially rich, professionally rich, and even spiritually rich. Richness, in my worldview, conveyed power, opportunity, attention, success, autonomy, and freedom in this world.

But there's a price to be paid for being rich in spirit like this as far as God is concerned. The price is a diminished heart or desire to be used by God. To be rich in spirit implies an attitude where, I presume, anything and everything I need can be provided by myself. Spiritually speaking, this is a dangerous place to be because Jesus said we only become truly rich in God's eyes by becoming poor in spirit.

The key to God's richest blessings and all the spiritual benefits He has in store for us hinges on our ability to see ourselves as we really are before God—*spiritually bankrupt*—in need of something we *cannot* provide for ourselves, humbly dependent on the goodness and the grace of the One and only One who can make us whole—God Himself.

Lost in my thoughts, Nick spoke up again, began to read the passage a third time, and asked, "What response is God asking you to make?"

I realized God was asking me what I was going to do with what He had just spoken to me about. In my case, I knew I had to take the next few days to search my heart for whatever treasures, *my riches,* were standing between me and a significant relationship with Him. God was calling me to focus on storing up treasure in heaven.

## You Can Take It With You

We began this book by asking you to ask yourself a dangerous question: "What treasure is standing between you and a significant relationship with God?" By now, you probably have a pretty good idea of what your *one thing* is, and it's our hope and prayer that by surrendering your treasure to God, you will be well on your way to the life of significance your heart has always longed for. But before we go, we want to clear up what we've found to be a confusing misconception among many Christians today. With regards to earthly treasure, we have all heard the reminder that "you can't take it with you." But Jesus said, the truth is, *we can take it with us*. In his Sermon on the Mount, in Matthew 6:19–21, Jesus told his disciples:

> Do not store up for yourselves treasures on earth, where moth and rust destroy, and where thieves break in and steal. But store up for yourselves treasures in heaven, where moth and rust do not destroy, and where thieves do not break in and steal. For where your treasure is, there your heart will be also.

When John D. Rockefeller died, a reporter at the press conference asked how much the multimillionaire left behind in his estate. Someone in the crowd shouted, "All of it!"

What a telling answer. Whether or not we can "take it with us" depends on what we're investing in and where our investments lie. Jesus said that the investments of our treasure will give us and everyone in our lives a crystal clear x-ray on the true condition of our heart. You see, when it comes to treasure, the heart is always the heart of the matter. Invest it only in your own agenda, your own stuff, your *one thing*, or some earthly kingdom . . . and you will, without a doubt, leave and lose it all.

## Taking a Second Glance

As you begin to recognize these signs of significance in your life—sacrifice, surrender, submission, simplicity, servanthood, surprise, and silence—you will find a life of significance well worth living. But the journey to a life of significance in God's Kingdom often involves taking the time to stop and take a second glance.

Pause to reconsider what God wants you to be and do in any moment throughout your day. God says that if you store up treasure in heaven by investing in His Kingdom—widows, orphans, the poor, the sick, the hungry, the lonely, the prisoner, and anyone with a need God is calling you to meet—you will realize dividends on such investments for all eternity.

We also hope this book has shown that your investments in God's Kingdom go far beyond the things we've just listed. Think about all the stories and the people you just read—people like you and me, who stopped to take a look at their lives and to take a second glance. . .

- What if Bonnie missed her treasure, which neither moth nor dust can destroy, by holding on to her secret and not allowing the truth to be told about her life? If she hadn't stopped and taken a second glance, would she have ever used her counseling gifts?

- What if Trish had followed what the world said was success, jumped in with both feet to a prestigious but overwhelming job, and not been able to give her children what they so desperately needed? Would she have the life of significance she has now?

- What if Rob had ignored God's nudging, kept his motorcycle, and settled for far less to give to those in need? From an eternal perspective, will he really miss his bike?

- What if the Rich Young Ruler had done what Jesus said? Who knows? To this day, we might have had the Rich Young Ruler Foundation for the poor.

True treasure doesn't start getting stored up after we get to heaven. Instead, we store up treasure in heaven while we are still here on earth. True, as we grow as followers of Christ, we do not always make the right decisions on the first try, but such decisions come more easily

- when we stop and take a second glance to consider what God truly wants from us as His followers

- when we allow His voice and the truth of Scripture to rein supreme in our hearts

- when we discover that a life of significance is well within our reach.

That could be the true measure of treasure—a second glance: to look at life from a Kingdom perspective, to take time to consider what we might be missing for eternity by not taking a step of faith today.

As you've read this book, we hope you've been challenged, inspired, and encouraged to do just that—to take a second glance. Look at your life now . . . and pursue a life of significance. Your life will reap rewards for today, for tomorrow, and for all eternity.

For updated information on the Kingdom Assignment
and to contact the authors be sure to visit our website:

www.kingdomassignment.com

*Are you ready for a Kingdom Assignment?*

# The Kingdom Assignment

### *What Will You Do with the Talents God Has Given You?*

DENNY AND LEESA BELLESI

The parable of the talents says that if I take what I have and give it to God, unlimited things can happen for others. Is this true? Does it work today? These are questions that are being answered in southern California at the Coast Hills Community Church in a nationally recognized way as the church leaders gave $100 bills to their church members and sent them out to do good.

Following a sermon on stewardship, Denny Bellesi stunned his congregation by distributing $10,000 among one hundred volunteers and sent them on a "Kingdom Assignment" that lit a spiritual blaze in their church, won the attention of the national media, and influenced hundreds of thousands of lives across their community and around the world.

There were three simple rules: The volunteers had to recognize that the money was God's money. They had to use it in ways that would extend His kingdom. They had to return in ninety days and tell what happened.

The results were astounding. The stories of how God blessed the creativity and faith of these kingdom recruits will move and inspire you. *The Kingdom Assignment* will stir you to big dreams, big faith, big deeds . . . and a much bigger vision of how God can use you.

Hardcover: 0-310-24323-8

## Pick up a copy at your favorite bookstore!

GRAND RAPIDS, MICHIGAN 49530 USA

WWW.ZONDERVAN.COM

We want to hear from you. Please send your comments about
this book to us in care of the address below. Thank you.

GRAND RAPIDS, MICHIGAN 49530 USA

WWW.ZONDERVAN.COM